More Marilyn

Other books by Marilyn vos Savant available from St. Martin's Press:

Ask Marilyn
The World's Most Famous Math Problem
"I've Forgotten Everything I Learned In School!"

More Marilyn

SOME LIKE IT BRIGHT!

The Best of the "Ask Marilyn" Letters Published in

PARADE

Magazine From 1992-1994

and Many More Never Before Published

Marilyn vos Savant

St. Martin's Press   New York

Production Editor: David Stanford Burr
Designer: Judith A. Stagnitto

Library of Congress Cataloging-in-Publication Data

Vos Savant, Marilyn Mach.
    More Marilyn / Marilyn vos Savant.
        p.   cm.
    ISBN 0-312-11384-6
    1. Questions and answers.   I. Title
    AG195.V667   1994
    031.02—dc20
                               94-21488
                                  CIP

First Edition: October 1994

10 9 8 7 6 5 4 3 2 1

This book is dedicated to
my mother
Marina vos Savant
with love and gratitude

CONTENTS

Part Three: Safety in Numbers

Part Four: Thinking and Feeling

Part Five: Questions That Need No Answer!

ACKNOWLEDGMENTS

What would I do without Walter Anderson, who inspires me, and without Sara Brzowsky, who never tires of striving for perfection, and without Larry Smith, David Currier, and Martin Timins, the people who make sure that the column is entertaining, educational, and correct? And what would I do without Richard Romano, who makes sure that no letter goes unread? (Well, I'd take much longer lunches, for starters.)

Dear Readers:

We've come a long way since the 1950s, when the phenomenon of Marilyn Monroe stressed beauty over brains and the highlight of a woman's career in politics was singing "Happy Birthday" to a President. Now it's the other way around—our minds are far more important than our looks. And from reading my mail, I see that young girls and older women alike are gaining immense inspiration from the women gaining this new stature in the world today. This is not something I could have ever foreseen when I began writing the "Ask Marilyn" column for *Parade* magazine eight years ago, and I'm proud to be a part of it.

Fiction writers sometimes have an experience in which their characters take on lives of their own and force the plot to move in unforeseen directions. Well, writing "Ask Marilyn" has been similar, even though my readers are real live people. (Don't miss the funniest questions in the last part of this book—I couldn't make up those letters if I tried!) The way I originally perceived the column and the way my readers perceived it turned out to be two different things entirely, but because what they ask determines what I answer, the twain did meet, and the result has been much more fulfilling, interactive, and successful than I could possibly have envisioned alone.

This is the second collection of "Ask Marilyn" columns; the first was published in 1992. The column has evolved over the years, and with age and experience come wisdom and proficiency. Like people, the column had an infancy, and I do view some of my early responses the way I view my baby pictures! It also had the "growing" pains of adolescence—there was an occasional fender-bender and resultant fight over the car keys—but the column appears every week now, and it soon found a healthy all-American identity. I now view "Ask Marilyn" as a well-adjusted young adult and, as with people, that comes from what our social scientists like to call a good "support system." At *Parade*, I have a loving family (my editors and the production staff), and I have dear friends and acquaintances (my readers).

Despite the importance of family, a circle of friends is even more vital— and what a vast circle "Ask Marilyn" has! *Parade* is the Sunday magazine for more than 352 newspapers in this country; it has a circulation of 36 million and a readership of 70 million souls. American readers even send copies overseas, and I've received mail from Central and South America, Europe, Asia, Australia, and Africa. (We haven't heard from Antarctica yet, but we haven't given up hope.) The column receives more than five hundred letters in a slow week, and sometimes twice that if a "controversial" response has appeared.

There's not enough room on the cover of this book to list all my co-authors (more than five hundred in this collection!), but I do want to thank them, as well as the many readers who have not appeared in print. All those letters have been important in building and shaping this column, and we're grateful for every one of them. (Well, now that I think about it, maybe I should take that back. I do remember a few that I could have done without.)

My experience as a columnist has taught me that you don't need complex and expensive technology to have an effective interactive media—a ballpoint pen and an attentive mind are all you really need, and my readers certainly have that.

Sincerely,

Marilyn vos Savant

Marilyn vos Savant
New York City
May 1994

Part One

One

LEADERS AND

FOLLOWERS

Dear Marilyn:
How can we find an *honest* politician?

Joe Waters
Hot Springs, Arkansas

Dear Joe:
We'll know we have an honest politician when the *winner* of a narrow election asks for a recount.

● ● ●

Dear Marilyn:
I realize that no one is perfect, so it is impossible to find the person who has not made his or her share of mistakes. Given this fact about human nature, I would like to know what characteristics you think are most important when considering who should be president of the United States. (Politics aside, of course.)

Michael Helfen
East Sandwich, Massachusetts

Dear Michael:
Another reason I believe we're not going to find a presidential candidate who has never made a mistake is that such a person would be far too indecisive to run for office, and we wouldn't want him or her, anyway. A country needs a leader, not a mouse.
And when we put politics aside, the decision is easy. Just listen to your heart, and vote for the man (or woman) that you'd choose to have as a father (or mother).

● ● ●

Dear Marilyn:
Political candidates usually promise that they will do certain things, but when they get into office, they don't follow through or the press finds some

kind of "wrongdoing" in their past. My question is: If a person ran for office and told the truth about what he hoped to do as well as about his past, could that person get elected?

Bruce Van Houten
Little Ferry, New Jersey

Dear Bruce:

I don't see why not, but here's what we might get: a timid individual (who never did anything in his or her life without approval) and an opinionated one, too (who makes early decisions and doesn't waver, even in the face of facts learned later). But at least we wouldn't wind up with an outright liar.

● ● ●

Dear Marilyn:

Are the sex lives of political figures fair game for the media? Personally, I don't much want to know, but if a wife can't trust her husband (or vice versa) in an issue as basic as marital fidelity, then I certainly don't feel we should trust that individual with issues of public policy. How do you feel about this?

Suzette Marie Couturier
Kent City, Michigan

Dear Suzette:

Regarding candidates for public office, I believe that anything true is fair game for the media, but I don't believe that marital fidelity is a black-and-white issue. Human behavior can't be judged apart from its context, and those people outside the relationship are the least likely to have the relevant information. For one thing, you assume that a spouse is worthy of lifelong devotion; not all are. And is the "other" person an individual of value, or not? Those two factors alone can make an entirely different scenario, and we can't neglect to consider them.

That is, infidelity may expose anything from a character flaw to a marital flaw, but the two aren't synonymous. Frankly, some of the finest people I know have been "unfaithful" to a marriage partner for one reason or another.

● ● ●

Dear Marilyn:

How can we get rid of the Electoral College so that the popular vote will elect the president of the United States?

Ottic Swain
Clewiston, Florida

Dear Ottic:

Whatever we do, we should look at the subject more carefully before taking the first step, in order to see if the result is what we really want. With the current system, the possibility exists that a president could be elected without a popular majority. (See next question and answer.) However, if we eliminate the Electoral College entirely, we could be faced with the prospect of the vote being spread among half-a-dozen different candidates, and a president could be elected with, say, only 20 percent of the vote!

● ● ●

Dear Marilyn:

I would like to know once and for all if it's mathematically possible for a United States presidential candidate to receive a majority of popular votes and lose the election due to the electoral process.

Louis Knight
Mascoutah, Illinois

Dear Louis:

Yes, it is, and it has already happened. Rutherford Hayes and Benjamin Harrison were both elected president with fewer votes than their rivals. And in modern times, the Carter-Ford race in 1976 is a good example of it nearly happening again. If Ford had received only some eight thousand more votes in Hawaii and twelve thousand more votes in Ohio, he would have won the electoral votes of those states and the presidency, but Carter still would have had a majority of the popular vote.

● ● ●

Dear Marilyn:

What are the incentives for the politicians who appear on television news programs so often? I doubt they sacrifice their Sunday mornings just to espouse their party's philosophy. Appearance fees could be significant. If so, are these controlled by any congressional rules?

Donald Barnes
Moreno Valley, California

Dear Donald:

There's no need. Neither politicians nor anyone else earns fees from interviews of that nature. There's a strong incentive, nonetheless. Considering how extremely expensive it is to purchase airtime, repeated appearances on these programs—without actually having to *pay* for them—earn the guest many millions of dollars worth of free publicity, advertising time for which other advertisers must pay dearly.

• • •

Dear Marilyn:

Why is it that the most powerful people in the world are usually quite insecure?

Roy Salins
Palm Beach Gardens, Florida

Dear Roy:

I don't think this is true. Apart from those with inherited power, such as monarchs, I think the opposite is usually the case.

• • •

Dear Marilyn:

Looking at all that's happening in the world these days, I have to wonder whether being a dictator is actually *more* stable than being another kind of leader. Look at Fidel Castro, for example. Or Saddam Hussein. What do *you* think?

Anonymous
Ann Arbor, Michigan

Dear Reader:

Appointing yourself "dictator for life" sounds secure until you realize the only method you've created for people to remove you from your position.

• • •

Dear Marilyn:

I've read recently that certain leaders in the Soviet Union may not be as bad as we thought and that Fidel Castro may actually be a diamond in the rough. I think it's possible, but what do *you* think?

Anonymous
Canon City, Colorado

Dear Reader:

I think your neurons must be napping. Some people may be diamonds in the rough, but others will never be anything more than a lump of coal.

• • •

Dear Marilyn:

Every day I become more convinced that the bad guys in this world have the edge over the rest of us and that they're taking over fast. The good guys just don't seem to have a chance anymore. Any ideas?

Michael Hanes
San Diego, California

Dear Michael:

Yes. Run for political office.

Two

G O V E R N M E N T

A N D   P O W E R

Dear Marilyn:

Was our government originally established as a democracy? I say it was, but my friend insists it was not.

E. S. Quinlan
Folkston, Georgia

Dear Reader:

Surprise! Your friend is right. The United States was founded by people with strong republican convictions, and this form of government was "guaranteed" in the United States Constitution. The Founders believed that laws, rather than popular approval, should be the final authority. The word "democracy" does not appear in the Declaration of Independence, the Constitution of the United States, or in the first state constitutions. Thomas Jefferson himself, often called the founder of the Democratic Party, said that he did not believe in government by majority and that he didn't trust "the mobs of the great cities."

● ● ●

Dear Marilyn:

I'm a Democrat, but I'd like to know how many times a Republican President has had a Republican Congress or even a Republican House or Senate to work with.

Jess Ceballos
San Diego, California

Dear Jess:

The Republicans haven't been able to get their way since Eisenhower's first term ended. Since then, they have never had control of the House, and they controlled the Senate only for a few years during the Reagan Administration.

• • •

Dear Marilyn:
Do you think we'd have a better system of government if lawyers were forbidden to participate in the formation of laws, and all laws passed were written by the average person?

Michael Simpson
Roanoke, Virginia

Dear Michael:
No. I think those laws would have more loopholes than a bathroom rug.

• • •

Dear Marilyn:
Do you think the government would purposely keep a cure for cancer a secret just because of overpopulation?

Maureen Reynolds
Patterson, California

Dear Maureen:
Not a chance in a zillion. Those people haven't even been able to manage to keep their *sex lives* secret.

• • •

Dear Marilyn:
What is the biggest reason why citizens hate to pay taxes?

K. P. Cooper
Alexandria, Virginia

Dear Reader:
Maybe it's that we've become so accustomed to government services that we take them for granted, forgetting their costs, and consequently feeling that we have suffered a loss in the transaction. When we feel bad about taxes, it might help us to remember that, in addition to such obvious benefits as schools, hospitals, and roads, the government provides the pervasive system of protection for a way of life in which we're able to earn an independent living at all. In other words, most of us are *products* of the system, however unwillingly, not *victims* of it.

• • •

Dear Marilyn:
Socialism is generally understood to be a socioeconomic system that benefits everyone equally. It has been tried several times and has been unsuccess-
ful. Capitalism is understood to favor the most productive people by
increasing wealth and providing for the less productive as a byproduct of
the system. Its shortcoming may be that it can lead to an unreasonable
imbalance of material things between the "haves" and the "have-nots." Is
there a system that is intended to both curtail poverty and increase wealth
as *equal* objectives?

R. E. Alexander
Erie, Pennsylvania

Dear Reader:
None that I know of—curtail poverty, yes, but increase wealth, no. However, there are all sorts of compromises, which you may or may not like,
between capitalism and socialism. One notable example is called "state
capitalism," which, in its classic sense, refers to a private capitalist economy
under the control of the state. To me, this means that instead of being
dominated by Big Brother, we'd be dominated by Big Bureaucracy.

• • •

Dear Marilyn:
What do you think is the best form of government? Plato thought that
democracy was the worst. If you think the best form of government is an
absolute monarchy, you have *my* vote.

G. L.
Washington, D.C.

Dear Reader:
Go back and read your letter again! (And I removed your name so you
wouldn't be embarrassed when you see that you should win this year's
"Internal Inconsistency Award.")

• • •

Dear Marilyn:
If there were no wars, would people be truly content?

Joe Sencaj
Windsor, Ontario, Canada

Dear Joe:

No. War is an *expression* of discontent, not the discontent itself. You don't rob a bank because you're content with the amount of money in your account.

● ● ●

Dear Marilyn:

What do think about television? Has it been good, bad, or indifferent in its influence and effect?

Walter Buell, M.D.
San Antonio, Texas

Dear Walter:

I think television has been rough on even the hardiest of us. It shows us beautiful people that we'll never look like, riches that we'll never attain, and excitement that we'll never experience. And no wonder, because so little of it is reality.

Breakfast with our *own* baby, for example—complete with orange juice on the wall, spoons on the floor, and cereal in the hair—can never match the final product of a film crew, three different kids to wear out, lighting soft enough to put a halo even on the dog, and eight hours of tape edited down to one perfect minute.

Three

POLITICAL

CORRECTNESS

Dear Marilyn:
Are you "politically correct"?

John D.
San Jose, California

Dear John:
No, I've never been that submissive. But I wouldn't call myself "politically *in*correct," either. "Politically impolite" is more like it.

● ● ●

Dear Marilyn:
What internal situation do you feel poses the largest threat to the well-being of the United States?

Kendall Cox
Haltom City, Texas

Dear Kendall:
Clearly, you're asking for a personal opinion, and without volumes of space at my disposal, that's all I can offer you on this subject. But here it is: Over the decades to come, one of the greatest threats to the stability of the United States may well be the decline in the number of people who call themselves Americans. I wonder how long the hyphenation of nationalities can continue without bringing the hyphenation of loyalties.

● ● ●

Dear Marilyn:
Is it possible for any U. S. citizen who is not an American Indian to avoid being hyphenated? Aren't we all from another country or the descendants of people from other countries?

David Carney
Birmingham, Alabama

Dear David:

We're all from other lands, all right, but that includes the American Indians, who probably came from northern Asia. And what about the rest of the world? Unless you believe separate populations of people sprang into being in different geographical areas, they *all* came from somewhere else— presumably the same place.

But let's say you simply feel that full-blooded countrymen should be defined as the people who settled first in a locale. That makes Spanish people native to the Galapagos Islands, Irish monks native to Iceland, and Americans native to the Ross Ice Shelf in Antarctica. (Unless you don't consider Richard Byrd, born in Virginia and a lifelong citizen of the United States, to be an American.)

And we can't ignore the British Isles and Europeans in this question. On the move throughout human history, settling and resettling, whom would you define as native to any particular geographical area? The Celts, for example, who originally settled England and France back in prehistoric times, were largely extinguished long ago. So, as no tribes of isolated English or French "natives" still exist, does this mean that there are no longer any Englishmen or Frenchmen and that the people living in those countries should be hyphenating their identities?

•   •   •

Dear Marilyn:

This is a very controversial subject among Mexican-Americans, of whom I am one. Most families teach their children first to speak Spanish and then English like a second language. From my observation, the children who are taught English first do better in school. Don't misunderstand me—I want to keep our heritage and ability to speak our native tongue, but I feel that when you're competing in an English-speaking country, your brain must not be slowed down by thinking in Spanish. I would appreciate your unbiased opinion on this heated subject.

Anonymous
Nogales, Arizona

Dear Reader:

I think there are times in life when school performance may be less important than cultural performance. However, this would vary according to the value system of each culture and even each family. I'd suggest that parents ask themselves this question when deciding what language to teach their children: How will my child feel about this when he's grown? Will he applaud my decision, or will he hate me for it? After all, it's the kids who will reap the greatest benefits and pay the greatest price.

• • •

Dear Marilyn:
I am of Native American and Irish ancestry. Recently I heard that many sports teams are changing their Indian-related name due to complaints from Indians that the teams' names were offensive. But would a team choose its name based on what it scorns or what it disdains? Wouldn't that team be more likely to choose a name based on what it admires and venerates? I have heard of no insulted Irish-Americans because of the Boston Celtics. Personally, I am honored that the Celtics were so named, and that Washington's football team is named the Redskins, and that Cleveland's baseball team is called the Indians.

L. K.
Medfield, Massachusetts

Dear Reader:
Your point seems well taken. If any of you Native Americans out there can enlighten me about your objections on this issue, I'll be happy to listen.

• • •

Dear Marilyn:
I have a natural preference for members of my own race, my national group, my geographic group, my family group, my political group, my religious group, et al. I try to manage this to conform to our cultural norms of "fairness," but I'm honest enough to admit it to myself and others. Don't you think "political correctness" has gone too far? Aren't we losing our right to free speech? Are "thought police" coming next?

Frank Powell
Florence, Alabama

Dear Frank:
I believe that yours is a benign sort of "discrimination" that is both natural and healthy, and that you shouldn't feel it's something you must call an "admission." It's the suffocation of that personal freedom that makes you feel caught in a George Orwell-style 1984. So please don't sound apologetic. But will "political correctness" become the American version of the Russian "Big Brother"? Good heavens, I hope not. We've always been too spirited for totalitarianism here.

Four

Dear Marilyn:

Although we hear about it every day, I don't suppose many could answer this question: To whom do we owe the national debt?

Carol Ann Slater-Murray
Fresno, California

Considering the huge debt our government has accrued, may we suggest it declare bankruptcy? It works for big business!

James Stadley
Magalia, California

Dear Readers:

Our politicians are doing a poor job of educating the public about the national debt. People might be more interested in applying the brakes to government spending if they realized that much of the national debt is owed to *them.*

Defaulting on a national debt usually occurs only after a revolution, when the new government repudiates the debt of the old one. In this country, federal bankruptcy would bring disaster to all who own government bills, notes, bonds, and other securities, including pension funds, and to the Civil Service Retirement Fund, the Federal Hospital Insurance Trust Fund, the Federal Old Age and Survivors Insurance Trust Fund, and the Department of Defense Military Retirement Fund, among others.

On the other hand, cautious retirement of the debt would likely eliminate the taxes required to pay interest and certain inflationary effects, and it would likely increase the rate of capital formation and business expansion.

● ● ●

Dear Marilyn:

These days we read so much about government programs costing billions and that the national debt exceeds $4 trillion! Personally, I have difficulty comprehending just how much a billion or a trillion is, and I'll bet most people do. Could you please give us examples showing the difference in a million, a billion, and a trillion?

Paul Blomgren
Spring Valley, California

Dear Paul:

One reason these numbers may be so hard to comprehend is that it is so hard to accept that our financial situation is this serious. Moreover, the real difference between a million, a billion, and a trillion is not so commonly known. They just seem like "a lot." But if you began to count dollar bills at the rate of one dollar a second, it would take you "only" 11.57 days to count to a million. At that same rate, it would take you 31.69 *years* to count to a billion. And at that same dollar-a-second rate, it would take you *31,688.09 years* to count a trillion dollars. The current debt is about four and a half times that much!

● ● ●

Dear Marilyn:

If every wage earner in the United States were taxed exactly 10 percent of his or her income with no adjustments, would the government receive more or less than it does now? Instead of going through the complicated and inequitable process that we currently have, would this be a more fair and simple plan?

Donna Blackman
St. Joseph, Missouri

Dear Donna:

The government would receive less. For it to receive the same amount, each tax return/payer would have to pay about 15.22 percent. However, this doesn't address the underlying issue. Should the government be spending that great a percentage of each taxpayer's income? And should there be so many taxpayers to begin with? Consider this: In 1914, the first year of the income tax, less than half of 1 percent of the population needed to file tax returns at all, and those people paid only $1033 each *in 1990 dollars.* Why?

These statistics isolate the growth of government. (The increase in population is discounted by using the percentage of people filing tax returns rather than the number of people filing, and the difference in the value of the dollar is discounted by using current dollars.) In other words, if today's government ran as parsimoniously as yesterday's government, most of us would pay no income taxes at all. Big Brother may not be here, but Big Democracy sure is!

• • •

Dear Marilyn:
How did the savings-and-loan industry lose $150 billion? Where did the money actually go? It doesn't just become lost, does it? Can you describe this catastrophe in simple terms?

Michael Darnell
Woodland, California

Dear Michael:
Much of the money isn't lost, but it's in the hands of ordinary people (and a few criminals) who don't deserve it.

The S&Ls came under pressure when interest rates paid by banks (and others) rose above their own rate ceiling, and they lost depositors; further, their loans were in long-term, low-interest mortgages. So they were deregulated. However, they then began to offer interest rates that were too high and took on too many high-risk loans; some people say that deposit insurance may have encouraged that behavior.

The S&Ls began to fail—largely because of uncollected loans, partly because people simply couldn't make their payments, and partly because the properties had declined in price. By 1986, the FSLIC had run out of money to back up the failures. The government subsidized the selling of many S&Ls to more secure institutions, but the rest must be bailed out directly. It also is estimated that fraud contributed heavily to perhaps a third of this mess, and surely sheer ineptitude characterized the rest of it.

After that column appeared, however, an anonymous reader wrote to add the following:

Dear Marilyn:
I am a federal financial-institution regulator, and, by government dictate, I cannot reveal my name or speak publicly regarding the debacle you addressed in your column.

While you touched on some of the issues, you didn't mention the ultimate cause of the problem—the high interest rates caused by inept economic policies of the late 1970s. These high rates caused money to flow from both S&Ls and banks to mutual funds. To counter, financial institutions were deregulated and allowed to offer competitive rates. Without deposit deregulation, all types of depository institutions would have failed due to an impending liquidity crisis.

. . . The fueling of this powderkeg was abetted by a totally incompetent regulatory authority. . . . If Congress had left this situation alone, very few S&Ls would have failed as more responsible fiscal and monetary policies in the early 1980s brought interest rates down to a manageable level. . . .

. . . You wrote that fraud contributed to one-third of the cost. Fraud did; but it was congressional fraud. . . . It also should be noted that current economic and fiscal policies will probably lay the groundwork for a repeat performance. Since the crisis, all regulatory agencies have lost their independence and are now being managed by Congress— the same Congress that fraudulently manipulated the S&L regulators before.

A Frustrated Bank Examiner

● ● ●

Dear Marilyn:

Can you give a definition of "inflation" and then explain the cause without just repeating the definition in other words?

Wallace Burton
De Soto, Missouri

Dear Wallace:

Open inflation is considered to be an undue rise in the overall level of prices, but there are probably numerous causes, which can all interplay to a greater or lesser degree, depending on the circumstances at the time. And then there are the variations such as pure inflation, gross inflation, creeping inflation, and galloping inflation. But most of us can console ourselves that we weren't in Hungary in June 1946, scene of the world's worst inflation, when the 1931 gold pengö was valued at 130 million million million paper pengös, and prices increased daily.

Five

WOMEN'S ISSUES

Dear Marilyn:

Why are women called a minority? According to the Census Bureau, there are more females than males.

Dave Powers
Syracuse, New York

Dear Dave:

The earliest and predominant meaning of "minority" is "the condition of being smaller, inferior, or subordinate." This is the origin of the word "minor" when referring to a person under legal age. Even if there are more of them in number, they're still minors. And as there's no doubt that women have always been subordinate, they are clearly a "minority" group.

If it were numbers that defined the term, we would call white people a world minority because there are fewer of them than, say, Asians.

● ● ●

Dear Marilyn:

Although women are valuable additions to the workforce (and they neither could nor would *want* to go back to their former roles), if men and women stayed in their traditional roles of "breadwinner" and "homemaker," wouldn't we have fewer whole families homeless? There will never be enough jobs for every able-bodied worker.

Marlene Yanchus
Wilkes-Barre, Pennsylvania

Dear Marlene:

In essence, then, you seem to think that perhaps women are gratuitously taking jobs that men could have to support women and children. If the situation were changed, presumably husbands would make money (with a bit of help from their wives), and wives would make babies (with a bit of help from their husbands). And that would perpetuate the system that totally blocked the entire female sex from historical prominence in the areas of politics, science, technology, literature, and the arts. The loss of half the contribution of humankind is a truly awesome price to pay.

Regardless, my answer to your question is "no." Your logic implies that we had full employment before women entered the workforce, but that clearly wasn't the case.

● ● ●

Dear Marilyn:
Sigmund Freud said that he had studied women for forty years of his life, and he still did not know what women want. Do you?
Bill Petty
Alexandria, Virginia

Dear Bill:
Asking "what women want" is really a question meant to trivialize their concerns by implying that they're never satisfied in some vaguely frivolous manner. Now, I won't blame *you*, Bill, but if Sigmund were doing the asking himself, I'd have no hesitation in telling him that what women want is what men want. They want respect.

I had no idea my reply would provoke the reaction it did. Here are just a few of the replies.

Dear Marilyn:
Your answer is inspiring and no doubt true for women in their public lives. But in their love lives? I'm not so sure.
Preston Woodruff
Brevard, North Carolina

Does respect include listening to women and no talking back?
Anonymous
Suburban Maryland

If women want respect, then why don't they follow the age-old saying, "If you want respect, you must give it first"?
Cliff Janis
Chicago, Illinois

I have been married to the same woman for the past forty years, and I have given her all my respect and almost everything else, and she has *never* been satisfied and is always whining and complaining about everything. Respect, my foot. They want everything under the rainbow.

Harry Moley
Charleston, West Virginia

What they really want is a contract registered in heaven, cut in stone, that they and their kids will never be hungry or in danger, and they expect men to give it to them.

Charles Wilkinson
Grand Prairie, Texas

Husbands are not particularly important. If they can't get along, the woman puts his blanket outside the door, and the man must collect it and slink off into the woods and out of her life.

Anonymous Man
Port Arthur, Texas

You almost had the answer, but not quite. The answer to the question is that women want sovereignty.

Jonelle Maison
Santa Fe, New Mexico

Good grief, it's tense out there.

●　●　●

Dear Marilyn:
I recently had a female customer with me in my car, and when I went to open the car door for her, she told me that it wasn't necessary. I was brought up to hold doors and pull out chairs for women. From this point forward, should I proceed as before, or should I forget this tidbit of chivalry? (In fact, she told me that "most" women in business resent this conduct.)

F. O.
Greenville, South Carolina

Dear Reader:
If I'm an invited guest in someone's home or place of business, or the like, I like being treated in a chivalrous way to a limited extent. I treat female (and male) guests the same way, myself. But when a man treats a woman as though it's a man's *world* and the woman is a guest in it, ushering her around as though he owned the whole darned city, it may not be well received.

The floodgates opened again. One woman even wrote, "Men may open the car door for me as a symbol of respect that I am of the superior sex. I base this on the fact that a city of a thousand men and one woman would do little in creating new life. However, in a city of a thousand women, one man, and a sperm bank, women could propagate our race. Let them open the door. Like in the military, we outrank them." (Notice that this reader felt she needed to add a sperm bank to the equation.) But most of the letters were from men. Here are just a few:

Dear Marilyn:

While I think it's wrong to treat a woman as though it's a man's world, we have a *world* of problems here. While on a date recently, I walked around my car to open the door for her, and during dinner, I was castigated at great length. Can we hear more from you on this? How are men supposed to act these days?

For males now there is the problem of seeming discourteous if we *don't* do these things (for some women) or perpetuating an outdated put-down if we *do* (for other women). I would really like to read your ideas on all of this. Please give us men some well-thought-out guidelines as you see them. And if you believe that this is not a serious problem, please think again. It is.

S. G.

Aurora, Colorado

Can you suggest any rules of thumb men can use to determine whether their actions might offend women? I strongly suspect these little actions cause more resentment than the big things. I greatly respect your opinion, and any light you can shed will be greatly appreciated by many bewildered men.

Donald Wert

Atlanta, Georgia

With regard to the lady who resented the gentleman opening the car door for her, I fully understand her attitude. However, I was brought up to do this, as well as to seat a lady, but from respect, not from macho ownership. Please do not suggest that I stop something that would upset my old Scottish grandmother.

Don Anderson

Bend, Oregon

Men are really taking a beating these days, all right. These guys clearly feel darned if they do and darned if they don't. But Grandma needn't worry; kindness never goes out of style. I can't speak for all women on this—no one can—so I'll just add how I feel privately and what I think might be the safest road to take. I like masculine, chivalrous behavior personally, but not

*professionally. However, if a cool professional relationship turns into a personal
friendship or even simply becomes a warm professional relationship with the
passage of time, I like it again. But that's just me.*

*For other women, I suggest two standards of behavior: one personal and
one professional. After all, you treat women one way when you're on a date,
but another way at the office. (I hope.) Given today's highly contentious (and
litigious) political and social climate, it's safer to desexualize the workplace
entirely, but on a date—why not treat women the way you'd treat your ideal
of a woman? And if she doesn't like it, you haven't lost much, have you?*

●   ●   ●

Dear Marilyn:

Please explain something that has baffled me for years. If males and
females are equal, and if there are as many females as males, why do females
allow males to dominate and *then* gripe about it? In my opinion, most females
seem to be masochistic and whiny, and I'm sick of hearing them complain.

Anonymous
Washington, D. C.

Dear Reader:

This is an important point. That is, if women are really equal, then how
could they have been dominated to begin with? The answer may be found
in women's role as nature's parent to the human offspring. Before birth
control was widely available, women were at a great disadvantage. Even
now, Mother Nature doesn't know anything about political correctness,
and women remain nature's only real parent. If they forsake that role,
there surely will be serious consequences; if not, they'll remain unequal,
at least as far as the workplace is concerned. But life takes place outside
of offices as well as inside them, and the workplace isn't the only honorable
place to be.

●   ●   ●

*I sometimes have answers waiting for questions, and this next fellow hap-
pened to ask me a question for which I'd had an answer more than ready.
Actually, this subject had been on my mind for most of my adult life, and I
was delighted to be able to reply in print at last.*

Dear Marilyn:

I've read that "vos Savant" is actually your mother's name. Why don't
you use your father's name?

John McCarthy
Lubbock, Texas

Dear John:
Never again, sir. Here's just a partial list of items that carry men's names: airports (John F. Kennedy), buildings (Trump Tower), cities (Cleveland), film companies (Metro-Goldwyn-Mayer), museums (John Paul Getty), racetracks (Churchill Downs), religions (Lutheran), rivers (Hudson), and I could fill page after page, including some of the most important corporations on the planet. All this makes sense to me, and men deserve this credit. However, I can think of nothing that women deserve to have their names on *more* than children. The injustice of this cannot be overestimated.

By now, we weren't surprised at the flood of mail that followed. Many women thanked me for putting their feelings into words, but some also wrote to stress that they were proud and honored to take their husbands' names. Tellingly, though, not a single man wrote that he'd be "proud and honored" to take his wife's name.

My "Least Favorite Letter of the Week" award surely goes to the man who wrote, "It is common knowledge that the man is the giver of life. The woman is the nurturer, just as Mother Earth nurtures the various seeds that impregnate her. Universally, agricultural offspring is referred to by the name of the seed from which it grew, not the dirt in which it grew. Human naming evidently followed from this eminently logical process." (It is tempting to include this fellow's name, but I don't want to feel guilty about what might happen to him after thousands of women read this!)

My real favorite read, "Why do I have the feeling that if your father's name had been 'vos Savant' and your mother's name had been something like 'Wienerschnitzel,' you would have chosen your father's name?" The following came next.

Dear Marilyn:
I have just read the column in which you give your reasoning for using your mother's name. I never before thought of it like that. Bravo to you for making us aware and for having the nerve to do so. Good for you, Marilyn.

75+
Fort Wayne, Indiana

There are plenty of things already named after women—ships, hurricanes, horses, and dogs are just a few.

William Reno
Sandy, Utah

Do you have something against your father? Why don't you wish to honor him?

Anonymous
Rockville, Maryland

But women have no names. They are only using names of males in their lives (either fathers or spouses).

Mickey LaCrosse
Shelton, Connecticut

Technically speaking, your mother's name really isn't her name, but her father's.

Faith Haynes
Garland, Texas

Dear Readers:

One at a time! My father (who passed away a few years ago) was an absolute dear; I loved him when he was alive, and I love him still. I took my mother's maiden name as an adult, and it delighted him. (And yes, I would have done it even if he *hadn't* been delighted.)

The argument that "women have no names" is selectively lopsided logic. Why do men have names, then? That is, if a woman doesn't have a name (because it's "her father's"), then a man doesn't have one, either (because it's *his* father's). And why should the fathers themselves be considered to have names? (They had fathers, too!)

If a male gets a name when he's born that becomes his own at that point, then a female gets a name when she's born that becomes her own at that point, too. So the logic of saying my mother's name "really isn't her name, but her father's" is just plain wrong. Why, you can use the same logic to say that my father's name "really wasn't his name, but *his* father's." It's the same either way!

And as far as honor is concerned, my mother is now finally getting what *she's* due. (Thanks, Mom!)

●   ●   ●

Dear Marilyn:

Why are the world's great chess players men? Is it male chauvinism or something biological?

Jack Martin
Red Bluff, California

Dear Jack:

I think it's psychological, not biological, but don't blame the men. Historically, women haven't put much effort into chess and where they have, they put it into "women's" chess, which I find an inexcusably repellent concept. Populated by so few women players, that type of chess has long been a much weaker version of the game, possibly even ruinous to those involved. But all that may be changing. As of 1991, the youngest grandmaster ever, surpassing even Bobby Fischer, is a Hungarian teenager—and a girl.

● ● ●

Dear Marilyn:
    Imelda Marcos still turns up in the news every now and then. What do you think of her life? I don't think it's been easy for her.
                                                        Bill Forder
                                                        Laguna Hills, California

Dear Bill:
    Of *course* it hasn't been easy for Imelda. How would *you* like to break in twelve hundred pairs of shoes? Even if she started back when she was twelve, that's a new pair of shoes every two weeks!

● ● ●

Dear Marilyn:
    I think ballroom dancing is one of the greatest things a man and woman can do together. But how can modern women stand dancing backwards most of the time? And having the man lead everything?
                                                        Doug LaVerne
                                                        Oak Ridge, Tennessee

Dear Doug:
    Oh, is nothing safe from the march of equality? Has it become "socially incorrect" to tolerate any difference in the behavior of the sexes? Should male ballet dancers begin to wear toe shoes? Is this really what we want?

● ● ●

Dear Marilyn:
    Do you think we'll ever go too far with women's equality? How will we know?
                                                        Teddy Moffett
                                                        St. Clair Shores, Michigan

Dear Teddy:
    When women are competing for 50 percent of the places on the "Ten Most Wanted" list, we'll know we've gone overboard.

Six

Dear Marilyn:
What is the most interesting topic on earth?

Krya Walter
Fort Worth, Texas

Dear Krya:
The future. What the stock market, your lover, and Iraq did last year is of far less interest than what they're going to do *next* year.

● ● ●

Dear Marilyn:
What is it that makes you decide how to vote?

Fred Smith
Memphis, Tennessee

Dear Fred:
For me, it differs from election to election. For citywide elections, such as those for the mayor, I'll vote for the person. For statewide elections, such as those for state senators and the governor, I'll vote for the issues. For most major elections, such as those for U.S. senators, and for nationwide elections, such as those for the president, I'll vote for the current party philosophy. (By the way, when I was younger, I rarely voted, using the excuse that my one vote didn't matter. But boy, have I ever changed.)

● ● ●

Dear Marilyn:
Is it unpatriotic not to "buy American"?

Robert Johnson
West Hartford, Connecticut

Dear Robert:
I don't think it's "unpatriotic" in the case of obviously superior products; that's what is best for unencumbered competitive forces working to create even better ones. (But they're seldom unencumbered, and that makes a big difference.) Either way, I don't see any need to use patriotism as an excuse to "buy American." Our products are clearly among the finest in the world.

● ● ●

Dear Marilyn:
Can individuals ever "save the environment" through individual actions? For example, isn't it true that most of the air pollution in our society is caused by major corporations?

Martha Hizer
Mystic, Connecticut

Dear Martha:
It may surprise you to hear that fully 50 percent of the air pollution in this country is caused by automobiles. Who do we think is driving them? And the next greatest source of air pollution is power-generating plants. Who do we think is using that power? Accepting some responsibility ourselves just may be the first step to finally taking effective action. I think individual effort can and will work, but only when there are enough of us ready to make some substantial sacrifices.

● ● ●

Dear Marilyn:
Why is our world the way it is today? Where did we go wrong?

Kristy Vinson
Olney, Maryland

Dear Kristy:
If our world isn't worth as much as it used to be, it might be the fault of all those who took more than they gave.

● ● ●

Dear Marilyn:
Please address a worthy question. With all of the dire problems facing humanity (to name a few: possible loss of the ozone layer, global warming, toxic waste, overpopulation), do you see any hope for us?

Art Riddle
Winston-Salem, North Carolina

Dear Art:

I'm more hopeful for the resolution of those first three problems, which were created by progress in science; I suspect scientists who are that advanced are up to solving them. I'm less hopeful, however, for problems created by widespread well-meaning but innocent attitudes toward childbirth and children. Continued population growth will surely result in the eventual devastation of other animal life and even plant life as well. Our once-vast forests are literally going up in smoke. If we don't change our values, life on a concrete planet, devoid of what we now know as nature, may be our reward.

●   ●   ●

Dear Marilyn:

What would happen if everyone on earth was absolutely equal?

Ed Broyles
Arlington, Virginia

Dear Ed:

Well, it would be really easy to get a date. But no one would care.

Seven

Dear Marilyn:

It's hard to feel safe anywhere you are, day or night, away from home. What are the statistics that a law-abiding citizen will be the victim of a crime?

P. Ignacio
Chesapeake, Virginia

Dear Reader:

In 1988, there were nearly 14 million serious crimes—which include murder, rape, assault, robbery, burglary, and theft. With a population of nearly 246 million, I suppose you could say this translates to something like 18 crimes per 100 people. However, you added the term "law-abiding," and that reduces your vulnerability greatly. Even the most careful printer gets ink on his hands.

● ● ●

Dear Marilyn:

I feel that there is a lot more crime today compared to when I was growing up in the fifties and sixties. My parents did not have the worries that I have with my children. My husband disagrees with me completely. He feels that because of television, newspapers, and the radio, we are just more aware of all the crime and violence. Who is right?

Rebecca Giles
Woodstock, Georgia

Dear Rebecca:

It's not just your imagination. I'm afraid you're right—and by far. Unless you want to believe that crime simply went unreported to the police in past decades, the truth is that in 1960, there were 1,887.2 crimes per 100,000 people (160.9 violent crimes and 1,726.3 property crimes); by 1990, that number had soared to 5,820.3 crimes per 100,000 people (731.8 violent crimes and 5,088.5 property crimes). That is, there is four to five times as much violent crime and almost three times as much property crime today (per person) as there was when you grew up.

• • •

Dear Marilyn:

If money were not a concern, and every person who committed a serious crime were jailed, how many people would be put in jail?

Jon Barrett
Allentown, Pennsylvania

Dear Jon:

I could simply recite the relevant statistics, but I know you mean something more than that. If we take organized crime as an example, it's an intriguing notion that if we actually jailed everyone who committed a serious offense, those who had committed *less* serious offenses might then be in a position to promote themselves and take their places. In other words, without a harsh judicial system willing to incarcerate everyone who does more than jaywalk, we might find that a criminal component is one of the many facets of a free society.

• • •

Dear Marilyn:

I'd like to hear your answer to this. "John" has broken the law all his life and gotten away with it. You name it—murder, robbery, and blackmail—John has always gotten away with it. Then one day, a murder was committed, and even though John didn't do it, all the evidence pointed to him, and he was convicted, sentenced, and executed. Was justice served?

I. Hartman
Delray Beach, Florida

Dear Reader:

Not in my book of rules, it wasn't. Justice seems to have been entirely absent. For example, who paid for John's crimes? Other "guilty" types? Entirely innocent folks? And even if no one was punished at all, what if John had been caught early on? He may not have had the opportunity to commit all the rest of those crimes. For the victims, where's the justice in that? So now we're left with one murderer on the loose instead of another. If he's no improvement on John, we haven't made much progress, have we?

• • •

Dear Marilyn:
    One is horrified to find that more and more school-age children and teenagers are using drugs and consuming alcohol. Why then are we not equally horrified that adults consume alcohol? What is the difference? Why is it illegal for children, yet legal for adults? Please explain.
                                    Michele Arceneaux
                                    Baton Rouge, Louisiana

Dear Michele:
    I am not justifying the use of any drug, including alcohol, but addressing only your point about two standards: one for children and one for adults. Are you suggesting that criteria of legality should apply equally to both groups?! That would mean either that schoolchildren should be allowed to work forty hours a week (like mature adults) or that mature adults shouldn't be allowed to work at all (like schoolchildren)! And what about sexual relations? Shouldn't the law distinguish between a six-year-old and a thirty-six-year-old?!

• • •

Dear Marilyn:
    Can you please tell me why, with all of the attention being given to equal treatment of both sexes, men are still considered less than second-class citizens in family court? I recently tried to obtain custody of my son, and even with a great track record, not only was I treated as an all-out idiot by the judge for even considering taking the child from his mother, I lost some of the rights I was given by the original judge!
                                    Philip Paonessa
                                    Danbury, Connecticut

Dear Philip:
    You can blame Mother Nature, who doesn't care about being "politically correct" and doesn't make the sexes equal, either. Studies show that male parenting is very rare in nature. Mothers are "born" (along with the baby) after a nine-month gestation period, complete with all the requisite hormonal changes and final construction from various biological blueprints. But fathers are "made." Men do whatever they want to do (influenced by such things as religion and local cultural practices), and that can range from spending one night with a woman (and never seeing her again) all the way to becoming "Mr. Mom."
    Men are capable of stepping in and doing a fine job in circumstances in which the mother is a poor parent, and they should be applauded for that

effort, but they can never fool Mother Nature and become mothers themselves.

• • •

Dear Marilyn:
I'd like to change my first name, but I don't know how to start. What do I do?

G. Kalem
Tacoma, Washington

Dear Reader
Although it's traditional in this country for a baby to be given the last name of his or her mother (if she is not married) or the name of the mother's husband (if she is married), it's no more than a custom—the latter left over from the women-and-cattle-as-property days. In general, you're free to just go ahead and start using your new name (first and/or last) with no legal formalities, assuming you have no nefarious purpose in mind. In addition, if you'd like, you can call your local courthouse and ask them to give their bureaucratic blessing to your decision. This is usually a very simple affair. I'd recommend it, however, because it will give you a piece of paper to use as "proof," the way your birth certificate had previously served as a means of identification.

• • •

Dear Marilyn:
When a picture is taken against the wishes of the subject, to whom does the picture belong? A friend of mine repeatedly tried to take my picture, and I repeatedly asked her not to. She did, it came out especially bad, and when I came into possession of it later, I was hurt by her insensitivity and kept it. She became very angry and spouted off about expensive film, etc. Was I right to claim possession?

Dorothy Huseman
Crown Point, Indiana

Dear Dorothy:
You probably weren't legally right, but I sure think you were morally right. The photograph itself belongs to the person who took it, and the rights of the subject are limited to questions of how it's used. Only if that use invades your privacy or makes a profit for someone do you have a complaint or a claim. (P.S. And I hope you got the negative, too.)

• • •

Dear Marilyn:
   Of the things he learns from books, what can a student honestly use as his own? Is it more ethical to copy word for word or to dilute and use?
                                                            Colleen Crowley
                                                            Fort Lupton, Colorado

Dear Colleen:
   This isn't a legal definition of plagiarism, but here's a good "working" definition for students writing papers that aren't for publication. Never take material from an open book unless you copy it word for word and give the author credit. If you write from a closed book, however, don't worry about it. That's the result of learning.

Eight

Dear Marilyn:

If you were allowed to make only one statement which your children would follow throughout their lives, what would it be?

P. G.
Rutherford, New Jersey

Dear Reader:

The length of your education is less important than its breadth, and the length of your life is less important than its depth.

• • •

Dear Marilyn:

As a former teacher, the term "overachiever" has always bothered me. I know what is meant by it, but I maintain that if you have *done* something—no matter how unlikely it was that you could do it—you have *achieved* your goal. Just what *is* overachievement?

Jean Burrows
North Catasauqua, Pennsylvania

Dear Jean:

I think "overachievement" describes an individual in relation to his peer group, not in relation to the individual's *own* goals in life. And in some cases, an "overachiever" seems to be a derogatory term for a person whose achievements have become self-congratulatory. But in other cases, the term looks a lot more like an expression of plain old envy.

• • •

Dear Marilyn:

I feel a real desire within to do something outstanding in my life. I'm not content doing everyday "routine" things. How can I find what I'm looking for? I've tried many fields, and I've had many successes, but this feeling is so strong.

Mary McDowell
Orange, Texas

Dear Mary:

My personal suggestion is that you look back over the fields in which you have experience, return to the one you enjoyed the most, and try to cultivate the art of patience! You sound like the successful type, but even changing one's professional focus *within* a field can be a temporary setback, let alone moving from field to field entirely.

● ● ●

Dear Marilyn:

If each person has his or her own special gift, should a person without a desired quality continue to strive for that goal or dream, or is it better to face reality and work with what you have?

Anonymous
Paterson, New Jersey

Dear Reader:

I don't really believe that's true, but even if it were, I think goals do far more for our character and for our world than gifts have ever done. Go for your dreams, dear reader, and let me know what happens.

● ● ●

Dear Marilyn:

How would you go about starting a career that you've always dreamed about but which seems very far out of your reach?

A. M. Pace
Chicago, Illinois

Dear Reader:

Consider yourself started. Making that inquiry was the first step. The next one is to find the most pertinent coursework to the field that you can and take a class. If, after finishing the class, you still don't know the next step, write to me again. (But I bet you will.)

● ● ●

Dear Marilyn:

I'm a high-school senior and torn between being an English teacher or a registered nurse. There is a desperate need for both here, and I'm qualified for both. I really want to be a teacher, but I think the pay and opportunity for advancement in nursing is greater. If you were me, what would you do?

Samantha Rumby
New Orleans, Louisiana

Dear Samantha:

You've spent plenty of time in schools, so you have some idea of what teachers do all day, but have you spent much time in hospitals? If I were you, I'd do some volunteer work there and talk to the nurses themselves. The less you like what you're doing, the more the opportunity for advancement diminishes.

● ● ●

Dear Marilyn:

I'm a freshman in high school and bright, but I have a fussy personality that can get in the way sometimes. That is, I like thoroughness and carefulness more than the average person. Also, I have a curiosity that never seems satisfied. Is there a career where my personality fits?

John Ritman
Highland Park, New Jersey

Dear John:

Sure! Take courses in biology, chemistry, physics, and the like. Science is obsessiveness at its most productive.

● ● ●

Dear Marilyn:

Am I in shock! I recently took the Law School Admissions Test and nearly blew it. This, after an academic career of straight A's and advanced degrees at prestigious universities! The LSAT presented logic puzzles and other types of questions that I had never been exposed to before. Does this mean that I'm dumb, after all, and that my grade point average is meaningless?

Shocked in Texas
Fort Worth, Texas

Dear Reader:

No way! It's been my experience that highly educated people who have difficulty with logic and the like have simply spent much more time learning *what* to think than they have learning *how* to think. It may be a deficit in your education, but it certainly isn't a deficit in *you*.

● ● ●

Dear Marilyn:

Performance anxiety greatly impeded my ability to learn during high school, college, and even graduate school. I am now, at age thirty-two, recovering from that state of perpetual panic. I've worked hard on my emotions and must now train my intellect. I want to learn how to think and how to learn. How would you attack this challenge? Are there books, courses, specific areas of study, or techniques that you could recommend? To learn, I know I must be unafraid to ask questions—hence, this letter!

Anonymous
Washington, D. C.

Dear Reader:

My suggestion is that you get into a classroom setting with a favorite subject, but preferably one that is as objective as possible. You'd like to learn "how" to think, not "what" to think, and elementary math courses are the best bet for training in logic and reasoning. More subjective courses such as art and literature do provoke less anxiety—but you've decided you want to conquer the problem of anxiety, not avoid it. And I think you've made a fine decision.

● ● ●

Dear Marilyn:

All through grade school into college, I never understood a math course, and so I took the bare minimum needed because I never could do better than a D. This year, I took a remedial math course (which included algebra and geometry) at night school and ended up with a B with almost no effort. Why did I do so well in a subject I had previously failed? (I did almost no studying and haven't looked at a math book since the age of nineteen.)

Bonnie Burnett
Royal Oak, Michigan

Dear Bonnie:

Congratulations! You may be living proof that our logic and reasoning ability can improve as we get older. Wouldn't it be interesting if we discovered that, because so few of us ever try math again, we just don't know how good we'd do?! (And I'll bet you didn't understand Shakespeare when you were a teenager either, did you? Well, you might now!)

● ● ●

Dear Marilyn:

A few years ago, one of the weekly magazines gave a list of books to read that would be equivalent to a college education. If you're familiar with this list, how would *your* list differ?

Beulah Hale
Richlands, Virginia

Dear Beulah:

I wouldn't make such a list at all because I'd never want to mislead anyone into thinking that a college education can be obtained from books. Thinking skills are acquired by interactive work with the subjects—not just reading about them. It's like trying to learn French by listening to cassettes. You'll know far more than you did before, all right, but it's nothing like living in Paris for four years.

● ● ●

Dear Marilyn:

I'd like to teach my students in the best way possible. What do you think is the most effective way to learn a subject—using a textbook, seeing a movie, being involved in a simulation, or a combination of all of them?

Arthur Skaer
Herndon, Virginia

Dear Arthur:

Speaking from personal experience, I'd say the best method is, well—personal experience! For example, when you're being driven around a strange city by someone else, you still don't have the foggiest notion where you are, even if all the landmarks are pointed out. But when you do the driving yourself, you'll learn more in a day than in all those other times put together.

● ● ●

Dear Marilyn:

Why can children under six years old learn with ease to name and identify the various kinds of dinosaurs from brontosaurus to tyrannosaurus?

Jerome Fink
Millburn, New Jersey

Dear Jerome:

Because we most easily learn what we like. Just try to get those same kids to remember the names of a dozen different kinds of bacteria! Can you envision a kindergartner saying, "Please, Dad, oh, p-l-e-e-z-e buy me a great big inflatable streptococcus for my birthday, okay?"

● ● ●

Dear Marilyn:

Why do we have to go to school and stay for six hours? Can't we just get tutors to come to our house for three hours?

Kevelyn Manning
Chicago, Illinois

Dear Kevelyn:

In special cases, tutors are the only alternative—but for *everybody*?! If there are thirty children in an average class, that means we'd need fifteen times as many teachers as we have now. But far more significant, our civilization here in the United States is so highly advanced that cooperative effort is no longer merely important; it is absolutely necessary. And learning intellectual skills in isolation has as many limitations, both for the individual and for the nation, as learning football skills in the backyard.

● ● ●

Dear Marilyn:

My younger brother and his wife are both schoolteachers, and they have a ten-year-old son who was born when they were in their forties. They drill this boy endlessly, and he has never ever been away from them. They take him everywhere—meetings, dances, and even adult parties. They tried very hard to enroll him into the school's gifted program, and he was finally accepted when he entered third grade. Now they're saying that this child is a "true genius" and that true geniuses are only born of older parents. Is this true? At what age do they develop their genius? (P.S. I don't have children of my own and feel sorry for this child. He talks and acts like a little old man.)

Name Withheld
Albuquerque, New Mexico

Dear Reader:

I've withheld your name. That poor kid. He's a victim of what I call "hyperparents," people who see a child as a chunk of raw material to be machined into whatever happens to please them—whether that's a genius, a major-league baseball player, or a prima ballerina. It can be done, all right, but it can't be done for long. Eventually, whether in two years or in twelve, the careful construction will begin to crack, exposing a real human being beneath. If he's lucky, that is.

● ● ●

Dear Marilyn:

My life is so boring. Sure, I attend jazz, ballet, violin, piano, karate, ceramics, drawing, belly dance, and modern dance. But it's the same thing over and over, and between all this, my parents are doing everything they can to make me smarter. I'm only in the seventh grade, and my dad is teaching me algebra. It's like they're trying to model me into the perfect child. Every time I try to tell them, they launch into this long lecture about how lucky I am. It's like I'm living two lives—actually, I can't think about anything except boys. We don't get any magazines unless they're educational. I can't have any friends over unless we're doing a project for school. My parents want me to read books only by famous writers like Dickens, but I like reading paperback mysteries. Sometimes I feel suffocated. I don't do anything except study, study, study, and practice, practice, practice. My dad is getting me science books for my medical degree that he wants me to get, and my mom is making me study for my SAT's. I need help! Any advice?

> M. L.
> Tempe, Arizona

Dear Reader:

I'll bet your parents will provide that help. Go to your mother and tell her that you know you're lucky, but you're beginning to feel just a little "too" lucky! How about suggesting this idea to her? Drop half of the lessons entirely and spend the money on paying for a few different friends (who can't afford it otherwise) to join you at the other half. A great deal of social skill is essential to professional success (not to mention personal happiness!), and if you're kept too busy to spend time learning that, all those lessons and cramming will be wasted.

● ● ●

Dear Marilyn:

Our fifteen-year-old son has been tested as "gifted" since age four, but he has little interest in excelling and is criticized by his teachers for not working up to his ability. The past two years have been *so* frustrating. Encouragement, positive reinforcement, pushing, and forcing are all useless. In your opinion, what are the chances of such a bright individual having a change of heart regarding his education and his future?

> A Worried Mother
> Harrisburg, Pennsylvania

Dear Reader:

I would say they're not good, and you should begin to significantly reduce your expectations for the degree of his success in life. This alone may help. And if it doesn't help *him*, it will at least help *you*.

● ● ●

Dear Marilyn:

As an educator, I'm interested in your opinion of "ability grouping" in the high-school classroom. Many parents of children who were formerly in honors classes are upset that the students in our school are now in mixed-ability groupings. Do you believe students should be homogeneously or heterogeneously grouped? This is a very hot topic in education right now.

Barbara Roosevelt
Clifton Park, New York

Dear Barbara:

I have mixed feelings about this subject, and I know I'll draw fire no matter what I say, but here it is. I think it's better intellectually for mainstream kids to be in mixed-ability groups, but it's worse for gifted kids. However, I think it's better socially for mainstream kids *and* gifted kids to be in mixed-ability groups. Moreover, I think the social aspect is more important than the intellectual aspect, both as they relate to personal happiness and success in life. And it's interesting that it's the *parents* who are complaining, not the kids.

● ● ●

Dear Marilyn:

I have been teaching English at a fine prep school for ten years. Unfortunately, I have seen the attention and focus of the school shift from academics to sports. I am not against sports, as evidenced by my having coached a varsity team for several years. But although our school recently built an expensive gymnasium, my frequent requests for a video camera for my public-speaking class have been turned down. As a result, I have begun to consider changing careers and have entered the doctoral program at the local university. I have mixed feelings about leaving, however, as I feel I would be abandoning my students and not truly doing my best to promote academics here. From your objective viewpoint based on this limited information, would you recommend placing commitment to cause before desire for personal growth?

Name Withheld
City and State Withheld

Dear Reader:

I'm not qualified to give personal advice, but let me offer my thoughts on the issue of duty that you raised. First, I find no indication that you ever *made* a commitment. If there weren't at least two parties involved, it was more of a private decision than a commitment, which can (and should) be open to continual reevaluation. Otherwise, you'd be a slave to every error you make. And if there was another party involved, was the commitment to *you* upheld? One-sided fulfillments make you a slave to *others'* errors.

And to what or whom would you feel obligated, anyway? The institution itself and what it stands for? That can't be. Or is it to the students? Well, you're not abandoning your students; each year, they grow, move on, and abandon *you*.

• • •

Dear Marilyn:
Have any studies ever shown a direct correlation between money thrown at education and the quality of education?

B. L. Morton
Glastonbury, Connecticut

Dear Reader:
I don't know of any reliable studies, but I doubt it. Does government improve by "throwing" money at it? Do people improve by "throwing" money at them? I think that "throwing" money at something just makes it *bigger*, not better.

• • •

Dear Marilyn:
Students commonly say that the work we're doing will never actually be used in our lives. What is your opinion on this?

Tammy Katy
Palm Beach Gardens, Florida

Dear Tammy:
I think that's often true, but that's not why you're doing it. Instead, you're laying a foundation of understanding the world so you can successfully accomplish the work you choose later on and not be a fool about how it (and you) fit into the overall scheme of things. If you're so narrow that you only know about what you do each day, you'll be both bored and boring.

• • •

Dear Marilyn:
Is attending an Ivy League school necessary for survival in the world?

Jiana Lopal
New York, New York

Dear Jiana:
Only to those who truly believe it is.

Nine

R E A D I N G   A N D

W R I T I N G

Dear Marilyn:
   How important is it to maintain a standard of using correct English in our society? Misuse really grates on me. Is it worth attempting to improve?

Jean-Marie Munday
Clovis, California

Dear Jean-Marie:
   I think it's very important, but for pragmatic reasons more than aesthetic ones. In a large population, the ability to communicate deteriorates rapidly without vigilance regarding the standardization of the language. Dictionaries are not a luxury; they're a necessity. Although only the most literate of us will take care to handle the language as well as possible, attentiveness to it may keep the uneducated from lapsing into limbo entirely. That is, a decline in standards not only may reduce our ability to communicate, it also may make that many more of us functionally illiterate. And that's a serious problem.

●   ●   ●

Dear Marilyn:
   When (and why) did the dictionary cease being a guide to correct pronunciation and become a guide to the most popular mispronunciation?

Evan Hopkins
Hastings, Minnesota

Dear Evan:
   I sympathize with your position, but I don't believe I can defend it. Dictionaries not only show "correct" standards for spelling, pronunciation, and meaning, they also show how those standards are constantly changing, and this has been the case throughout history. (The *Oxford English Diction-*

ary, in fact, is universally praised for tracing the history of every word and its changes over time.) Otherwise, we'd all be speaking "pure" Latin and Greek and all the other ancient (and unrelated) languages.

• • •

Dear Marilyn:
   What foreign language should we study to help us most to improve our English?

Ardis Watkins
Helena, Montana

Dear Ardis:
   Latin, I suppose—but why not just take advanced courses in English? Knowing the origins of words is helpful, of course, but there's no substitute for great English literature.

• • •

Dear Marilyn:
   It's important to be able to communicate a message that is understood, but why must a person be able to tell if a word is a noun, pronoun, verb, adverb, adjective, and so on? What is to be gained from learning how to diagram a sentence? I really think far too much emphasis is put on this aspect of learning English grammar.

Edward Jacob
Holland, Indiana

Dear Edward:
   Oops, you've bumped into an advocate here. Diagramming sentences over and over and over is what eventually gave me a completely clear grasp of the structure that underlies grammar, and I think it's one of the most important exercises in early schooling. Because diagramming is so logical, it makes the rules far easier to understand, and I can't recommend it highly enough.

• • •

Dear Marilyn:
   Is the sentence "I don't know where I'm at" considered correct English? If not, what is the rule concerned with the placement of the word "at"?

Tabitha Yothers
Falls Church, Virginia

Dear Tabitha:
   As far as I know, English has no prohibition against the use of a preposition at the end of a sentence, even though the word "preposition" itself means "to come before." And losing points on a grammar exam is something out over which I would be put.

● ● ●

Dear Marilyn:
   In a presentation, I said, "It was news to my partner and me." Afterward, several people told me I should have said, "my partner and I." I was correct, but I'm sure most of the audience believed I had used poor grammar. Next time, should I purposely say it the wrong way so my listeners won't think I'm ignorant?
                                                Timothy Klein
                                                West Carrollton, Ohio

Dear Timothy:
   If you do, I'll bet even more people will tell you that you should have said it the other way. Worse, they'll be right! Anyway, people who have the gall to "correct" without knowledge of the facts aren't people you should worry about impressing.
   As for myself, I've broken grammar rules on purpose—for humor or special effect. One example was the time I wrote, "All humidity levels are not created equal," a play on "All men are created equal." (And yes, I received letters of complaint.)

● ● ●

Dear Marilyn:
   You once wrote, ". . . a physical therapist has every right to be delighted when *she* sees her stroke patient take *his* first halting step down the hall." If these pronouns were reversed, your female readers would scream male chauvinism, so allow me the same opportunity to holler feminist bigotry.
                                                Leonard Scaletta
                                                Anaheim, California

Dear Leonard:
   People write about this sort of thing routinely. As everyone knows, the word "he" has long been traditional in many contexts. But if I use "he," people write and accuse me of continuing male chauvinism. And if I use "she," people write and accuse me of forcing feminism down their throats. As I'm not going to be intimidated by people who can't see that you can

argue it either way, I'm just going to continue to do what I think is best and then toss the letters in the wastebasket.

• • •

Dear Marilyn:

Aren't we making a fuss over nothing in using words like "chairperson" as a replacement for "chairman"? After all, the primary definition of "man" is "a human being." Doesn't this mean these words aren't sexist in their current forms?

Mike Palombo
McMurray, Pennsylvania

Dear Mike:

When we say "man" alone, we're probably referring to a member of the human race, all right, but when we say "a man" or "the man" or the equivalent, we're referring to a male. So the "man" in "chairman" ("a chairman" or "the chairman") and the like would belong in the "male" category, not the "human" category. This usage is a serious social statement to many people, and calling the attempt to change it "a fuss" (in an effort to trivialize their concern) is a good example of how we use language to form opinion.

• • •

Dear Marilyn:

Exceptional speakers and writers aside, which form of communication do you think is clearer—verbal (where the speaker has the use of tone, gestures, feedback, etc.) or written (where the author has the opportunity to reflect and revise)?

Ross Meyer
Fort Worth, Texas

Dear Ross:

Judging on the issue of clarity alone, I'd pick verbal communication for nonfiction and written communication for fiction. If I'm trying to understand information, for example, I'd much rather hear the author explain it to me personally. But unless he or she is actually reading a script, I sure wouldn't want to sit and listen to anyone attempt to tell me a novel.

• • •

Dear Marilyn:

Why do we feel we must quote someone other than ourselves when talking about an issue?

P. H. P.
Chandler, Arizona

Dear Reader:
   Those who feel that way either lack confidence in themselves or are speaking with others who lack that confidence. And unfortunately, one often causes the other.

● ● ●

Dear Marilyn:
   When I bring a quote to class, my teacher won't accept something like, "I'll never go farther than my own backyard," with Judy Garland as the quoted person. She wants to know who *wrote* it, not who said it. But I feel that once someone gives a quote to an actor or a politician, he gives up that credit. The class has been feuding with her over this. What do you think?
                                             Maureen Gallagher
                                             Chambersburg, Pennsylvania

Dear Maureen:
   I agree with your instructor that we must be careful to give credit where it's due, but we shouldn't give a writer *undue* credit, either. Historically speaking, I think a quote belongs to the character who spoke the line because his or her stature was what made it memorable; the same sentiments expressed by more ordinary people go unnoticed. That means, "And so, my fellow Americans, ask not what your country can do for you; ask what you can do for your country" should be credited to President Kennedy, but, "I'll never go farther than my own backyard" should be credited not to Judy Garland, but to *Dorothy*, whose role gave it meaning.

Even after all these years, my readers continue to surprise me. I've gotten used to disagreement, but I haven't yet gotten used to the kind of item that generates it. The following column was the result of the mail that followed.

Dear Marilyn:
   John F. Kennedy stole those words, and history should *not* credit him with such a profound and beautiful line. The words were those of that great black American, Booker T. Washington.
                                             Elizabeth Kilpatrick-Cantine
                                             Ocala, Florida

   The credit should go to Justice Oliver Wendell Holmes.
                                             Amy De Vries
                                             Omaha, Nebraska

Lady Bird Johnson is the one who said it.

Gloria Rowlette
Seminole, Florida

President Warren G. Harding said it many years prior.

Robert Williams
New Orleans, Louisiana

Actually, the author is Kahlil Gibran, the mystic poet.

Frank Blacha
Fairbanks, Alaska

Shouldn't the proper credit go to Cicero, the Roman orator?

Joseph David Gregory
Lomita, California

It was Adolf Hitler!

Cynthia Nicolini
Baytown, Texas

Dear Readers:
Has anyone considered Elvis Presley, maybe?

●   ●   ●

Dear Marilyn:
As a professor of history and geography, I am confused about why the media and some officials call us—the citizens of the United States—"Americans." America is the name of a *continent*, not a *country*.

Alexander Bowen
Gretna, Louisiana

Dear Alexander:
I'm afraid it may be for the same reason that we call the grand finale of our baseball season the "World Series." We think we're the only ones who count.

But I was wrong about that one. And very pleased to hear about it, too. This next letter appeared shortly afterward.

Dear Marilyn:
May I offer an alternative explanation? We are the only nation in the world whose official name includes the word "America." Every other nation

in the New World, from Canada to Argentina, has a specific name that doesn't include that word.

Bernard Bobb
Pullman, Washington

Dear Bernard:

Thanks! That makes good sense. Now I can feel even better about calling myself an American!

By the way, quite a few readers wrote and maintained that the first "World Series" was sponsored by a newspaper called The World, *which gave the series its name. However, I've been unable to confirm that. It's my understanding that the first World Series was held in 1884 and it was known as the World's Championship Series; the name was shortened to World's Series and then, in 1903, to World Series. So, in the case of professional baseball at least, it appears that maybe we* did *think we were the only ones who counted.*

• • •

Dear Marilyn:

A long time ago, I read in a crossword puzzle book that there were only three words in the English language that ended with the letters GRY. I know about anGRY and hunGRY, but what is the third word?

Jacqueline Garwood
Fort Worth, Texas

Dear Jacqueline:

There's a word spelled "aggry" that has been applied to a kind of ancient glass bead found buried in Africa, but I've certainly never heard anyone use it. I know of a fourth word too, by the way, but it's obsolete, and the most recent reference I can cite was in 1603, which was, "She was delivered of a pale, meagry, weake child, named Sicknesse." Now, that's a woman with a bad sense of humor!

But it didn't quite end there. See the next letter.

Dear Marilyn:

I was very happy to read your answer of "meagry" because that was one we did not have in our ready reference file here at the library. Someone once gave us another word, "puggry." However, I suppose we would have to consider that Hindi rather than English.

Suzanne Sutterfield
Columbia, Georgia

Dear Suzanne:

I think it should be included in the list of words ending in GRY, bringing the total to five (not counting the word "gry" itself). The reason I didn't include "puggry" (a type of head-covering worn by Indian natives) the first time is because the *Oxford English Dictionary* doesn't spell it that way, although "puggry" is, indeed, one of more than half-a-dozen variations of puggree. Those variations also include "puggaree," "puckery," "pukree," "pugree," "pugaree," "puggri," "puggery," and "pagri." So now we can be better prepared to say things like the following, quoting a gentlemen from 1845: "The Mohamedan Belooch always obeys him who wears the Puggree."

• • •

Dear Marilyn:

Is there a word to describe a series of letters that spell one word forward and a different word backward? Examples are desserts/stressed and diaper/repaid and reward/drawer.

Mrs. M. H. Baird
Annandale, Virginia

Dear Reader:

This was the original meaning of the word "anagram," which has now broadened to include all transposition of letters. Today, "palindromes" cover that narrower territory of words that read backward and forward. A "recurrent" palindrome reads *different* words forward and backward, and a "reciprocal" palindrome reads the *same* forward and backward. Reciprocal palindromes can stretch into sentences. This is one of the most famous: A man, a plan, a canal: Panama. And there's even a 30,000-word novel called, perhaps not surprisingly, *Dr. Awkward and Olson in Oslo*.

• • •

Dear Marilyn:

Why is it that "tongue-twisters" can be so difficult to pronounce? That is, why do we get confused over simple words?

Jeannie
Granger, Indiana

Dear Jeannie:

I don't know. And here's one from real life that I ran across while paging through one of those little mail-order catalogs. Try to say it quickly without looking at it.

HIS AND HERS SHOE SACHETS

(No, I can't say it, either!)

• • •

Dear Marilyn:
   What should be the correct form of the plural for "fax"? Being a fairly new word, dictionaries are of no help yet. I maintain that the plural of fax should be "fax," if only for euphonious reasons; "faxes" just grates on my ears.
                                                                    Lib Shore
                                                                    Loxahatchee, Florida

Dear Lib:
   I cast my vote for "faxes," anyway. It may not sound exactly *good*, but at least it sounds better than "taxes."

• • •

Dear Marilyn:
   Recently, my friend came to my house with a bakery bag. He stated that it contained fresh doughnut holes and that he would let me have them all for fifty cents. Knowing a bargain when I see one, I quickly gave him the money. Glass of milk in hand, I opened the bag to nothing. When I demanded a refund, my friend restated that the bag contained exactly what he said it did—holes. Does he owe me a refund?
                                                                    Dolores Scott
                                                                    Washington, D. C.

Dear Dolores:
   I think he owes you a bagful of doughnuts. His argument is full of "holes"! You don't use a bag to carry "nothing," and a bakery bag routinely carries little pastries called "doughnut holes," which are what he clearly stated it held. But if he honestly believes in interpreting language literally, the bag would have to hold *entire doughnuts* to be able to justify calling any spaces "doughnut holes" and not "mouse holes," for example! (And he shouldn't be surprised to order a hot dog at a baseball game and be handed a thirsty cocker spaniel.)

• • •

Dear Marilyn:
   My mother went to a dinner party and before she left she said, "Don't move before you take the garbage out." Now, how can I take the garbage out when I can't move?
                                                                    C. Carlson
                                                                    Brainerd, Minnesota

Dear Reader:

You just can't, kiddo. So I suggest that you spend the entire evening sitting at the table like a cabbage, waiting for her to return. And that means no television, no telephone, and no snacks. I bet that'll teach *her* a lesson, huh?

Part Two

Ten

Dear Marilyn:
 Which is more important, food or sex?

> M. L. B.
> Washington, D. C.

Dear Reader:
 Food. But if you didn't know that before, I doubt that you're going to believe it now!

● ● ●

Dear Marilyn:
 Does the same type of food, if fixed the same way, taste the same to every individual person?

> Michele Austin
> Roanoke, Virginia

Dear Michele:
 No, it varies. In addition to physiological differences that make some people experience the four basic tastes (bitter, salty, sour, and sweet) more or less strongly, taste also depends on our particular capacity to smell, our individual nutritional needs, and even what sort of saliva we have. So the next time someone makes a face at your potato chip dip, don't rush out for cheese and crackers. (Wait until someone actually *suggests* it.)

● ● ●

Dear Marilyn:
 If cholesterol is a problem, should eggs be eliminated from the diet?

> B. Barnes
> Troy, New York

Dear Reader:

Even if you were allergic to only the yolk and could never eat another one, why would you eliminate the rest of the egg? Foods like peaches and avocados and olives have *stones* in the middle, and you don't complain about *them*, do you?

•   •   •

Dear Marilyn:

I recently heard about a study that suggests that chocolate abuse can be inherited. Have you heard anything about that?

Vernetta Hayes
Plainfield, New Jersey

Dear Vernetta:

Spare me the details, Vernetta. There has been so much money squandered on so many dumb studies that the next thing you know, someone will spend a million dollars to discover that *money* can be inherited.

•   •   •

Dear Marilyn:

According to an answer on a television game show, curly black hair is dominant over straight blond hair. This doesn't square with personal observation. Did someone goof?

D. A.
Duluth, Minnesota

Dear Reader:

Nope, that's right. And brown eyes are dominant over blue eyes. But here are a few heredity surprises: Nearsightedness or farsightedness is dominant over normal vision; a nervous temperament is dominant over a calm temperament; and short stature is dominant over tall stature. (And where have you been doing this observation of hair, anyway? Scandinavia?!)

I was amused to then receive letters reminding me that Minnesota is indeed populated by a significant number of people of Scandinavian descent—hence the name of the football team "Minnesota Vikings."

But more important, my comment about Scandinavia was facetious and wasn't meant to imply that because a trait is dominant, it will also be more common. Nature doesn't work quite that way. For example, the piebald trait that produces a white forelock of hair is dominant, but it is rare in the population.

●   ●   ●

Dear Marilyn:
    If it is true that hair is "dead," how does it know when to stop growing? If your legs are shaved, the hair grows to a given length and then stops.
                                        Linda Simkins-Ruane
                                        Oceanside, California

Dear Linda:
    Oh, hair is dead, all right, but the follicles that produce it aren't. They operate in cycles of a given length (depending upon the area of the body), which means that each hair produced will grow to a certain length and then stop. Cutting the hair doesn't affect them; if you shave your legs and then inspect the area closely over the next few days, you'll see that some of the hairs get longer, and others don't. And fortunately, follicles don't operate as a team even when they all live in the same neighborhood—our heads, for example—or we would all become bald every few years!

●   ●   ●

Dear Marilyn:
    Recently, a cousin asked me, "How does a painkiller pill know enough to go to your right shoulder to relieve the pain there and not go to your left knee or whatever?" I got bogged down trying to come up with an explanation. Can you help?
                                        William McClurg
                                        Lake Placid, Florida

Dear William:
    The various analgesics, from mild to strong, all act in different ways, but the oral ones have at least one aspect in common. They have a systemic effect, which means that they don't just go to your right shoulder—they go *everywhere*, including your left knee, even if they aren't needed there. But if you don't have pain there, you just don't notice it as much.

●   ●   ●

Dear Marilyn:
    I understand that antibiotics don't kill germs or bacteria. So what *do* they do?
                                        J. Rice
                                        Long Beach, California

Dear Reader:

There's such persistent misunderstanding about what antibiotics can and cannot do that we really should try to clear it up. One, they don't act against viruses; and two, they *do* act against bacteria. That action *can* be killing them or at least inhibiting their growth. Knowing this, if we start using the terms "viral infection" instead of "a bug" and "bacterial infection" instead of "germs," it'll be less confusing all around.

● ● ●

Dear Marilyn:

Can a cold originate in a person, or does it have to be spread?

Calvin Dean
Dothan, Alabama

Dear Calvin:

It has to be spread—even if by someone who is having no symptoms. And you can't catch a cold from cooler temperatures themselves; Arctic explorers are remarkably free of them. However, colds are indeed more common in the winter, perhaps from drying conditions indoors or from reduced resistance outdoors. So, when your mother tells you to "bundle up so you don't catch cold," she may be right.

● ● ●

Dear Marilyn:

Can you comment on the belief held by some that smelling a putrid odor might cause you illness because the source of the smell has actually entered your body (in some small degree) via your nose?

Richard Gardiner
Granite Bay, California

Dear Richard:

Throughout history, people have believed that diseases were caused by "miasmas," the odors that arose from decaying vegetation in swamps. This isn't too surprising, given the contagion through "breath" of many illnesses— certain forms of the plague, for example. And bacteria do, indeed, get trapped in the nose, although many are destroyed there. In other words, the nose works as a defense mechanism.

The sense of smell, however, is said to be ten thousand times as sensitive as the sense of taste, so it seems more significant in this case than it actually is. That is, although we may be inhaling some of the source of an odor, all right, we're inhaling precious little of it, and even the stench of a packing-house won't give us a disease.

• • •

Dear Marilyn:
Who develops more problems with vision—the person who reads a lot and does much close-up work or the more physical person, like an athlete?
Sherrie Sundquist
Spokane, Washington

Dear Sherrie:
Neither reading all night nor running all day will affect a person's vision, because nearsightedness and farsightedness are related to the structure of the eye. However, reading excessively may fatigue your eye muscles temporarily, just as running too much may tire your legs. Eyestrain won't cause you to become nearsighted or farsighted, but if it's happening too much, it could be a sign that you already need glasses, anyway.

• • •

Dear Marilyn:
What part of the brain is used when we dream?
Hariette Nichols
Swansboro, North Carolina

Dear Hariette:
We use just about the whole brain when we dream. Embarrassing, isn't it? It would have been nice to blame all that nonsense on a spot the size of a ladybug.

• • •

Dear Marilyn:
I've heard that you grow at night. That isn't true, is it?
Bobby Dawes
Roanoke, Virginia

Dear Bobby:
In a way, it is. You can "grow" a quarter of an inch or more in your sleep, but you shrink back down after you get up in the morning. At night, the spinal discs expand because you're lying down, but during the day, gravity compresses them back to your usual upright self. For a similar reason, astronauts on long space flights can be as much as two inches taller when they return to earth. (But not for long.)

• • •

Dear Marilyn:
People who have flown across the country know that a five-hour flight can cause jet lag. In 1990, two men flew the SR-71 Blackbird across the country

in sixty-eight minutes. Was their jet lag greater, equal to, or less than that of a person who took five hours to make the trip?

Warren Loveless
Bethesda, Maryland

Dear Warren:

Assuming they didn't turn around and come right back, it was the same. Jet lag is caused by the time-zone adjustment, not the length of the trip itself. Regardless of whether you drove around your own city for five hours or for sixty-eight minutes, you wouldn't have jet lag at all. The reason people often feel much better when they take a supersonic flight to Europe, is not that they've cut the travel time in half. Rather, it's because they've avoided the regular flights that usually travel at night, during which time passengers must attempt to sleep while bent into the shape of a paper clip, causing them to be exhausted by the time they arrive at their destination.

● ● ●

Dear Marilyn:

Why does the human stomach not digest itself?

Jeff Scott
Indianapolis, Indiana

Dear Jeff:

The interior of the stomach is coated with a very thin layer of neutralizing mucus, only a millimeter thick, and it's thought that this protects the stomach itself from the powerful gastric juices it contains.

● ● ●

Dear Marilyn:

Is it physically possible for me to swallow a mouthful of water while standing on my head?

Milton Hoffman
Denver, Colorado

Dear Milton:

Why are you concerned, Milton? Are you going to be hanging around with bats? Yes, it's possible, although it may take you several swallows to mechanically move the water upward against gravity. A greater number of us face the more common obstacle of swallowing a very *cold* liquid, like a frozen drink. A frigid beverage can slow down or even stop the movement in the esophagus necessary to swallow, giving rise to the momentary feeling that your ice cream cone is hovering somewhere above your collarbone.

• • •

Dear Marilyn:
    I am puzzled as to the differences in how our bodies "feel" temperature. When the weather is in the seventies, we think it's a pleasant day, but when swimming, the water temperature must be higher before it feels comfortable. Why?
                                        Fran Wyman
                                        Riverside, California

Dear Fran:
    Because water can cause you to lose body heat more rapidly than air. Water is much denser; it can absorb a great deal more heat, and it can do it much faster.

• • •

Dear Marilyn:
    My wife often is cold while wearing a sweater, while I can be in the same room and be warm without wearing a sweater. Why do people vary so much?
                                        Steve Held
                                        Santa Rosa, California

Dear Steve:
    There's so much individual variation here, ranging from complex metabolic differences to circulatory interference to simple adaptation, that it's impossible to say. But here's an experiment in adaptation that you might enjoy. Place one hand in a bowl of hot water (about 104° F); at the same time, place the other hand in a bowl of cold water (about 68° F.) Keep them there until they've adapted to the temperature. Then place them simultaneously in lukewarm water (about 86° F). Amazingly, the "cool" hand will feel warm, but the "warm" hand will feel cool!

• • •

Dear Marilyn:
    Why, if the human body temperature is about 98.6° F, does an outdoor temperature in the low to middle nineties feel so warm? In other words, if I'm 98.6° F *inside* my skin, why should I feel too warm when the temperature *outside* my skin is *less* than that?
                                        Larry Mahon
                                        Panama City Beach, Florida

Dear Larry:

I hope you don't take this too personally, but are you wearing any clothes, Larry? Aside from such considerations as wind and humidity, your clothing insulates you so successfully that you'll feel warm in it. You can prove this to yourself by taking off all your clothes when it feels like a perfect 72° F outside. (Then again, maybe *inside* would be better.)

● ● ●

Dear Marilyn:

We spend the first months of our life in a human body where the temperature hovers around 98.6° F. How do babies stand that kind of heat twenty-four hours a day every day for nine months?

Raymond Bishop
Springfield, Illinois

Dear Raymond:

They dress for the climate.

● ● ●

Dear Marilyn:

Why can't you tickle yourself?

N. Riley Heagerty
Oswego, New York

Dear Riley:

Oh, but you can! Ticklishness is a sort of "spot" reaction to a threat. If you're ticklish on the soles of your feet, try gently running your fingernails along them. You'll feel only the most minor discomfort—that's the real biological tickle—and not much else, because you know you aren't being threatened. But if an enemy holds you down and does the same thing, you'll become agitated; you certainly won't laugh. Laughter arises only when you're tickled by someone you know doesn't threaten you, and you're amused by the feigned aggression. (Those of us with older brothers know this from firsthand experience.)

Consider what it feels like to grab yourself around the neck. That's not too exciting. And when a friend jokingly pretends to strangle you, you'll laugh—but if a hidden stranger leaps out at you from an unnoticed doorway and tries it, you'll react wildly.

● ● ●

Dear Marilyn:

My boyfriend does not have a ticklish part on his body—and I've tried just about everywhere. Is it possible that some people are not ticklish at all? Help, I'm running out of spots to try.

Anything But Tickled Pink
Sacramento, California

Dear Reader:
Hmmm. A small number of people aren't ticklish at all, but I'm always suspicious when it's a boyfriend!

• • •

Dear Marilyn:
My husband, who is six feet tall and weighs two hundred pounds, can do fifty pushups. I am five-feet-two and weigh a hundred pounds, and I can do twenty-five pushups. He says that because he does twice the amount of pushups at twice the body weight, that he is twice as strong! Is he correct?

Helen Shearrow
North Canton, Ohio

Dear Helen:
Frankly, Helen, I wouldn't argue with the guy, if I were you. Let him think whatever he wants!

• • •

Dear Marilyn:
If a 150-pound man expends a certain amount of energy to walk one mile on a flat surface on a windless day, will more or less energy be expended if the same person rides a bicycle along the same route under the same conditions? It would seem to me that due to friction within the bicycle, contact with the road, and wind resistance, the only advantage would be time saved for the rider at the expense of additional energy. I have friends who disagree.

Virgil Sams
Bandon, Oregon

Dear Virgil:
The man would save both time *and* energy. Spending calories at the normal rate of 210 per hour for each of those activities, he would travel about 5½ miles bicycling, but only about 2½ miles walking. This means that to travel just the mile you mentioned, he'd expend only about 38 calories on his bicycle, but about 84 calories on his feet—more than twice as much.

• • •

Dear Marilyn:
Is evolution within the human species continuing to occur?

Vicki Brown
Madison, Wisconsin

Dear Vicki:

If you mean the kind of evolution that is most easily seen in the fossil record, no. It appears to have been arrested—at least temporarily. Among other reasons, culture has come between the human species and its environment. In short, mankind is in the process of being tamed.

This is not to say, however, that the human species is no longer changing within itself. For example, a particular blood type could become predominant in the gene pool, but that doesn't lead to a new species. On the whole, we *are* what we *were*.

Eleven

Dear Marilyn:
How many animals on earth keep only one mate for life?
Vincent Tesi
Staten Island, New York

Dear Vincent:
Ah, not quite all of them . . . I mean, not all that many of them . . . that is, pretty few, actually. To be perfectly frank, hardly any at all! In nearly all mammals, the male mates with numerous females because he does not serve a parental role. And even many of the animals that we like to see as monogamous—certain species of birds, for the most part—are only together for one mating season, after which, they, well, fly the coop!

•   •   •

Dear Marilyn:
My elementary-school teacher stated that only humans could see color. Was she correct? If not, could you give examples of various living things and the ranges of colors each can see?
Ray Rowe
Beaverton, Oregon

Dear Ray:
Not all animals are color-blind. Primates like chimpanzees have color vision nearly equal to that of humans, and plenty of other animals can see in color too, although not as well as we can. Dogs, for example, can readily distinguish red, violet, and blue, but have trouble with yellow, green, and orange. (In humans, this used to be called "green blindness.") Even insects see color, although to quite a few of them, leaves are yellow!

• • •

Dear Marilyn:
Do fish sleep?

H. R. Hirleman, M.D.
Cedar Rapids, Iowa

Dear Reader:
Not really. All fish are different, and many get listless regularly, but none of them have true eyelids, so our accepted definition of sleep doesn't apply to them very well. (When I was a child, a member of my family used to tell me that he sometimes slept with his eyes open, and I almost believed him—until I leaned over his bed one morning, made a silly face at him, and he laughed.)

• • •

Dear Marilyn:
How are schools of fish able to change direction so rapidly and all at the same time? Is there really a lead fish?

Lynn Langston
Golden, Colorado

Dear Lynn:
Well, it's not *quite* at the same time, but we humans don't share in this ability, so it's difficult for us to comprehend. Fish use a set of extremely sensitive nerve cells that run in a lateral line across their bodies. These neurons detect minute changes in water pressure from side to side, signaling each fish to turn this way or that almost instantaneously, depending on what the rest of the fish are doing. There's no First Fish, however; the Steering Committee is whoever happens to be in the front.

• • •

Dear Marilyn:
Do fish feel pain when caught on a hook?

Stella Hoffman
Edison, New Jersey

Dear Stella:
Despite the fish's apparently desperate struggles, this is hard to say. Responsiveness to touch is a property of all life, and even a one-celled organism will withdraw from it. Be we can't assume that all such movement is equivalent to human pain. Consider this: If a person has met with an accident, and his spinal cord is severed, he'll have no feeling whatsoever—

neither pain nor pressure—below the affected area. But if we sever the spinal cord of a fish, something quite different occurs. In response to what would seem to be a painfully intense pinch of the tail fin, the upper part of the fish seems similarly unaware, but the lower part of the fish "writhes." Because the two parts are isolated, this gives rise to the interpretation that the fish's movement actually may be an adaptive motor reaction rather than a manifestation of suffering.

And fish are not an oddity of nature. Some animals show no signs of human "pain" at all. The dragonfly, for example, will even eat its own body with apparent comfort when its tail is brought into contact with its mouth.

•   •   •

Dear Marilyn:
    Why do we fear insects—animals that are less than one one-hundredth our size? We can easily step on them, and it's all over.
Chuck Rosene
Elgin, Illinois

Dear Chuck:
    I don't know, but size isn't the only consideration. Bacteria are tiny, but they can be very dangerous indeed. So can certain insects, and maybe that has a subconscious effect on us. The hidden number of insects also may be an underlying concern. If insects ever got together and ganged up on us, they'd not only outnumber us, they'd even outweigh us. For every human being, it is said there are about *twelve times* his or her weight in insects!

•   •   •

Dear Marilyn:
    How many times can a mosquito bite a person before he is too full to take another bite? I just had a sleepless night getting repeatedly bitten by a mosquito who kept eluding me, and I wondered if it was really the same mosquito.
H. M.
Port Richey, Florida

Dear Reader:
    Make that "she." As far as we know, only the female has the equipment to bite and suck blood, and she uses it to produce the eggs out of which wiggle all those cute little baby mosquitoes. One big drink is all she needs to last her for days, but it takes her a fair amount of time to get her straw properly inserted, and if she's interrupted, she'll just persist until she gets either tired or swatted, whichever comes first.

• • •

Dear Marilyn:
Why doesn't a spider get stuck in its own web?

Clem Harris
Jacksonville, Florida

Dear Clem:
This isn't completely understood yet, although one reason given is that spiders may coat their legs with oily substances. But there are too many different kinds of spiders and webs for a brief answer, anyway. In addition to the familiar trap-door spiders, which open silk "trap doors" at night to catch insect passersby, many other spiders capture their prey in curious ways. One Brazilian species heads out to a likely spot and erects a web in the middle of the night, then detaches it like a tent at sunrise, folds it up neatly, and carts it back home to open it picnic-style, with breakfast already conveniently stuck to the tablecloth. Another tropical species builds a little web about the size of a quarter and throws it over passing insects like a net.

• • •

Dear Marilyn:
Why do birds sit on electrical wires?

D. Barker
Salt Lake City, Utah

Dear Reader:
I can think of two reasons: (1) Wires are a convenient addition to the world's supply of tree branches, and (2) birds would fall over if they lay down on them.

• • •

Dear Marilyn:
How can birds keep their feet from freezing when they sit on a heavy wire when it's twenty degrees below zero? They do have blood in their little feet, and it seems almost impossible that the circulation rate could be fast enough to help.

E. F. Reiner
St. Paul, Minnesota

Dear Reader:

Among other things, birds have a special circulatory structure that actually makes their legs operate at a lower temperature than the rest of the body. This is one of the reasons that penguins don't have to dance around on the ice to keep warm.

• • •

Dear Marilyn:

If I find a baby bird on the ground, should I return it to its nest?

P. K. Compton
Lexington, Kentucky

Dear Reader:

In general, we should leave baby birds alone unless they've been injured (in which case the local wildlife agency should be contacted), but not for the reason most folks think. The mother will not reject the baby just because it has been touched; birds don't even have a strong sense of smell. Instead, there's a good chance that a baby bird on the ground is simply learning how to fly; the mother is likely to be nearby and watching over the situation. Our "help" could cause distress or even injury.

And who are we to interfere, anyway?! How would you like it if you were sitting in the backyard, showing your baby how to drink from a cup, and a well-meaning bird flew over and dropped a worm into its mouth?

• • •

Dear Marilyn:

I've had a parrot for about twelve years in a small candy store near a school, and children and grownups used to come in just to talk to him. He had a vocabulary of about thirty words and even whistled, mostly at the ladies. Today, it's just he and I, and he doesn't talk too much any more. Not long ago, someone told me that he has no brain and can't think for himself. Is this true?

Stephen Kraus
Jersey City, New Jersey

Dear Stephen:

Heck, no. Just because his speech is mainly mimicking behavior, that doesn't mean he's stupid. You guys just need a little more company these days. Your parrot friend certainly does have a brain and can think perfectly well, even if not as well as humans can. I'll bet he never whistled at a chunk of rock candy, did he?

• • •

Dear Marilyn:
How does a chicken in an egg get its oxygen? I've heard that eggs are porous, but what good does that do when a bunch of feathers are sitting on them for a month? People can be smothered with feather pillows. And how about turtle eggs that are covered with two feet of sand?
Priscilla Atwood
Hendersonville, North Carolina

Dear Priscilla:
The developing chick doesn't actually begin to breathe until the day before hatching, and before that, it just doesn't need very much more than what Mom already has provided. Soon after the egg is laid, air begins to penetrate the shell, accumulating in that space between the two membranes at the large end of the egg. The shell is resistant to the evaporation of stored water, but allows oxygen to diffuse into the egg and carbon dioxide to diffuse out of it. Other than that, it's a closed system and doesn't need much more than warmth and safety. So the feather comforter isn't a problem, but if a fertilized egg is immersed in water for a long period of time, almost completely depriving the inner environment of oxygen, the baby chick can "drown"!

• • •

Dear Marilyn:
I've never seen turkey eggs on sale. Are they edible? There are plenty of turkeys around. What happens to the eggs?
Herman Lunse
New York, New York

Dear Herman:
Turkey eggs are used only for making more turkeys, because the eggs themselves taste gamey, you can't fry or scramble them worth a darn, and they're expensive, too. (But none of those details stopped the caviar producers, did they?!)

Oh boy, did I ever goof on that one, and this next reader let me know it. The following column was the happy (if time-consuming) result.

Dear Marilyn:
As Vice President of Consumer Affairs for the National Turkey Federation, I agreed with most of your response to the question concerning turkey eggs,

but it is not true that eggs from domestically grown turkeys have a gamey taste. In a blindfold test, I think anyone would be hard-pressed to distinguish a flavor difference between a chicken or a turkey egg. The truth is that they're not practical for commercial use. They're very expensive (one egg can cost over seventy-five cents), and in this country, they're not inspected for human consumption.

Teresa Farney
National Turkey Federation
Reston, Virginia

Dear Teresa:

I'm embarrassed. You'd think we'd have known better than to take other peoples' word for it—even that of several experts—but we did. We were disparaging about turkey eggs without even trying one first! Not that it's all that easy to get one, understand. After thirteen phone calls, here's a sample of what our efforts produced:

(A nearby national grocery store) "Turkey eggs? No, doll. Turkey eggs? Let me give you up front. (Yells.) Where can she get turkey eggs?"

(A small local grocery store) "We don't handle turkey eggs. Get hold of one of those health stores. Or maybe Bloomingdale's."

(Bloomingdale's) "Turkey eggs?! No. Try Dean & DeLuca's."

(Dean & DeLuca's) "My manager just stepped away. Call back and ask for John."

(Balducci's) "Hello, meat. Turkey? A whole turkey? Try Ottomanelli's. But we could get duck eggs."

(Ottomanelli's) "No, I'm sorry. They're pulling your leg."

(A poultry company) "Let me ask somebody. (A long pause.) Have you checked with a live poultry?"

But the National Turkey Federation sprang into action and rescued us by delivering two dozen farm-fresh turkey eggs right to our door. For a good first impression, I personally took a couple of them to a favorite neighborhood restaurant the next morning where Sammy, the head chef, fried them "sunny-side up" for me for breakfast. And I'm happy to report that I was wrong! My eggs were delicious—mild and smooth—some of the best fried eggs I've ever had!

But we wouldn't stop there, would we? My assistant at the time, Sharon, took a couple of eggs home with her, and her friend Rick scrambled them. "They're terrific, delicate—it's amazing," they said. And I even boiled two more myself—exhausting my cooking skills—and my husband was equally pleased.

And so here's a big "Thank you!" to Teresa at the National Turkey Federation for setting the matter straight. And knowing how this lady operates, we're certainly going to avoid ever making unkind comments about the turkeys themselves, if we can help it. I don't want to walk by the mailroom someday and hear gobbling inside!

• • •

Dear Marilyn:
  I know that crossbreeding within the cat family and within the dog family is common. For instance, my peek-a-poo pup is the offspring of a Pekingese and a poodle. Would it be possible for you to inseminate a cardinal with the sperm of a blue jay, making a beautifully patriotic red, white, and blue bird?

Ellen Fanchen
Lovington, Illinois

Dear Ellen:
  With my luck, Ellen, it would come out *purple.*

• • •

Dear Marilyn:
  Why do bats hang upside down?

Jamie Lynn
Worcester, Massachusetts

Dear Jamie:
  Because of the way they're built, bats can perch upright only for a few moments at a time. But don't worry. Their circulatory system is well equipped to handle their upside-down roosting, and just as all of our blood does not rush to our feet when we stand, neither does all of their blood rush to their fuzzy little heads when they hang.
  All in all, in fact, bats are managing their affairs very well, thank you. It may surprise you to hear that they now comprise the second largest order of mammals in the world, outnumbered only by rodents. (And we thought *mousetraps* were unpleasant to handle!)

• • •

Dear Marilyn:
  How do bats sleep all day upside down, then fly all night rightside up? If I tried that, I'd be dizzy, with nosebleeds and headaches! What's so special about bats?

Ernie Tarret
Greenville, South Carolina

Dear Ernie:
I don't see anything so special about it. After all, you sleep *sideways* at night, don't you?

• • •

Dear Marilyn:
Whoever got the idea that horses needed shoes?

Marvin Brasch
St. Louis, Missouri

Dear Marvin:
It must have been whoever noticed that when horses were domesticated—substituting an artificial, man-made environment for a natural one—their hoofs wore down dangerously fast. In the wild, horses are perfectly well equipped for life, but when they're forced to carry loads or walk on paved roads, getting around is considerably tougher on the tootsies. However, despite the accommodation of shoes, female horses, at least, may be lucky. After all, no owner has yet been dumb enough to think that putting high-heeled horseshoes on them would better attract the male horses.

• • •

Dear Marilyn:
I've heard that in the wild, a tigress and a lion do mate, as do a lioness and a tiger, and the offspring are called ligers and tigons. Is this true?

Rita Scoles
Oxnard, California

Dear Rita:
Sort of. It doesn't happen in the wild, but zoos have been known to force the issue. (Forgive me. I don't often get a chance for such a bad pun.) And like mules and hinnies, ligers and tigons usually are sterile.

• • •

Dear Marilyn:
Is it possible for a cat and a rabbit to breed successfully? I once saw a picture of a cat that had the hindquarters of a rabbit. Then yesterday, I saw a friend's cat run; it hopped like a rabbit, and its hindquarters looked exactly like a rabbit's!

Marjorie Monroe
Chiloquin, Oregon

Dear Marjorie:

No, I doubt that there's ever going to be a market for catnip lettuce. The basic unit in biological classification is the species, the members of which can mate with each other and produce offspring, usually fertile. (On the other hand, crossing a horse and a donkey, which are of different although closely related species, produces either a mule or a hinny, both of which are nearly always sterile.) But cats and rabbits are not even closely related species in the same genus. And they aren't classified in the same family, the next higher rung on the ladder, nor even in the same order, the next higher rung above that.

Quite a few readers wrote after that answer, certain that the reader had seen a Manx, which is a tailless breed of cat with longer hind legs than forelegs. That's likely, but the lady may know a Manx when she sees one, and the existence of Manx cats doesn't answer her question.

● ● ●

Dear Marilyn:

A friend and I have been arguing relentlessly over the question, "Why do dogs have tails?" She says they're for protection of that area of a dog's body; I say they're either for balance or expression. Which is it?

Lucy Frembgen
Madison, Wisconsin

Dear Lucy:

I think *you're* right. But it may not have always been that way. The upturned tail, ranging from a coil to a broad arc, has been a physical feature of dogs only since they've become domesticated. In addition to smaller, less-powerful teeth, the "friendly" tail is one of the major noticeable differences between a dog and a wolf.

● ● ●

Dear Marilyn:

Do dogs dream?

David Weisman
Boston, Massachusetts

Dear David:

Evidence shows that dogs (and other mammals) do have the dream state of brain function while asleep. In one study done back in the 1960s, monkeys were trained when awake to press a lever whenever they saw a visual image on a screen. When asleep, they continued to press the lever during "dream" sleep, but not at other times. But what in the world would dogs dream about? Padding down the sidewalk and suddenly discovering, much to their embarrassment, that they had no fur on?

•   •   •

Dear Marilyn:
I heard that chocolate has something in it that a dog cannot digest. Is this true?

Gordon Nickman
Homedale, Idaho

Dear Gordon:
Yes. Worse, it can be lethal. In addition to caffeine, chocolate contains a substance called theobromine, another central-nervous-system stimulant. Although the caffeine alone can be a problem for dogs, the theobromine can be a killer. The maximum amount of chocolate that a dog can consume before symptoms develop is only .04 ounces of baker's chocolate or .4 ounces of milk chocolate per kilogram (about 2.2 pounds) of body weight. At that rate, a twenty-two-pound dog can consume no more than .4 ounces of baker's chocolate or 4 ounces of milk chocolate without becoming ill, and a 1-pound box may well kill him or her.

•   •   •

Dear Marilyn:
I've been hearing about a theory that states that if all human beings adhered to the practice of vegetarianism—instead of eating other animals— it would alleviate the problem of world hunger. But wouldn't the amount of the total land area that would have to be cultivated be detrimental to our all-important deserts and forests?

George Hamilton
Long Beach, California

Dear George:
An important desert?! Deserts are the barren *result* of using land too intensively (in addition to unavoidable climate changes) and are the dreaded consequence against which we must guard—not promote! But more to the point, it is indeed already a practice for people in overpopulated areas to increase their food supply by eating grains instead of animals that eat grains. However, this will *not* serve the cause of those animals, which is the driving force behind much of vegetarianism, the way it is often assumed.

Here's why. The total energy supply in the form of grains in those areas is partly consumed by the animals just in living. When the animals are eaten, the people don't obtain all the energy that the animal ever ate. They acquire only the difference between what the animal ate and what the animal used. Therefore, people can get more energy from the same food supply simply by eating the grains themselves, bypassing the animals entirely. But don't get the idea that this protects the animals; it doesn't. With their food supply eaten by people, they starve.

Twelve

Dear Marilyn:

People used to believe that the sun revolved around the Earth, and that the Earth was flat. Anything to the contrary was considered absurd. Today we know these ideas are incorrect. Isn't it naïve and egotistical to think that the "facts" we're teaching our children today are correct? We must be wrong about a few things that have simply not yet been disproved. What kinds of things do you think these might be?

John Geoghegan
Lexington, Kentucky

Dear John:

I agree with you, and I think the first theories in physics and cosmology to meet a timely demise will be those theories that everyone "believes" but few people (if any) really understand. (It's very difficult to "understand" a theory that is wrong.)

● ● ●

Dear Marilyn:

Why do the environmentalists wring their hands about the hole in the ozone layer when the weathermen always list ozone as one of the major pollutants?

Florence Amass
Sarasota, Florida

Dear Florence:

Like the sun, ozone is fine at a distance, but you don't want it in your front yard. In short, there's "good ozone" and "bad ozone," depending mainly on where it's located. Ozone is very irritating and can even be toxic to human beings in high concentrations down here in the lower atmosphere where we live. In the upper atmosphere, however, it acts as a very important barrier against excessive solar radiation.

● ● ●

Dear Marilyn:
I don't know how seriously to take the situation about global warming. When I hear about things like using spray cans less, I wonder. I'm just a farmer. How could I be personally concerned?

Abraham Tuttle
Franklin, Indiana

Dear Abraham:
Here's just one example. Global warming experts now are saying that the average cow belches up to four hundred liters of methane gas every day, and methane is twenty to thirty times as potent as carbon dioxide in trapping heat.

● ● ●

Dear Marilyn:
If cities and forest fires can create their own weather, can strong and unusual weather contribute to its own endurance? That is, can the weather create its own weather?

Anonymous
Eugene, Oregon

Dear Reader:
As smoke particles from fires may reduce rainfall and thus promote continued dryness, giving rise to more fires, so too can weather alone sustain and amplify itself. For example, early snowfall increases the reflectiveness of the ground, which retains less solar energy afterward, which encourages more storms to follow it, dropping more snow.

● ● ●

Dear Marilyn:
I recently purchased a home that is at the highest point in the development, although it is not the highest house, and I found out that the chimney had been struck by lightning. Is it likely to happen again? Is a lightning rod a good idea? Should I be worried?

Thunderstruck
Frederick, Maryland

Dear Reader:
  It sounds like you already are! Yes, it may happen again, and a lightning rod, which works by diverting the current through the path of least resistance down into the ground, is a good idea. However, a lightning rod only provides protection in the shape of a cone, so depending on the size of your house, you may need more than one.

● ● ●

Dear Marilyn:
  If the temperature rises from 1° to 2°, is it twice as warm?
                                                    Robert Kopec
                                                    Forty Fort, Pennsylvania

Dear Robert:
  No, because temperature doesn't begin with either zero degrees Fahrenheit or zero degrees Celsius.

● ● ●

Dear Marilyn:
  My question is about the effect of the wind-chill factor on a machine, such as an automobile. My son and I have had numerous discussions on this subject, and my stand is that a machine does not understand the wind-chill factor; it only understands temperature. I hope you can resolve this long-standing dispute.
                                                    J. Giammarinaro
                                                    Easton, Pennsylvania

Dear Reader:
  Actually, this is complicated, and you both may be partly right. Is the car sitting in the driveway, or is it running? The wind-chill factor is a rough measure of the cooling effect of wind (on humans), but another way to express that is heat loss. In general, warm-blooded creatures are generating heat to lose, and inanimate objects (such as a rock) aren't, which means the latter are not affected by wind-chill. However, if you're warming up the car for a cold-morning drive, it's a different question to consider.

● ● ●

Dear Marilyn:
  In the phrase "relative humidity," to what is the humidity actually relative?
                                                    John Tashjian
                                                    San Marcos, California

Dear John:

It's related to how much moisture the air can hold at its current temperature, and that's the point that causes most of the confusion. All humidity
levels are not created equal. It's a common misunderstanding that a relative
humidity of 70 percent in the summer (when it's warm) is the same as a
relative humidity of 70 percent in the winter (when it's cool). But this isn't
so. The same relative humidity in summer is *more moist* than in winter
because warm air can hold more water vapor than cool air.

● ● ●

Dear Marilyn:

Our wives were discussing the difference in baking bread in Denver and
in the Gulf Coast area. I said there was a difference in the temperature at
which water boils for the two elevations; therefore the difference in baking
time. Our friend's husband said it was the humidity. We would like *your*
answer.

C. D. J.
Taylorsville, Utah

Dear Reader:

Keeping in mind that high-altitude baking and high-altitude cooking are
two different things, we'll concentrate on the former. Because of the lower
boiling temperature of water at high elevations, the cake will not brown as
easily, so the oven temperature is increased. And because of the reduced
barometric pressure, more water will evaporate from the cake, so water is
added to the recipe. And for the same reason, the cake will also rise more,
so flour is added on a rainy day. (You guys should have just asked your
wives.)

● ● ●

Dear Marilyn:

Honey poured from a container will diminish in dimension and seemingly
in proportion to the distance it falls. Why? It seems that it should remain
the same.

William McCraney
Huntington Beach, California

Dear William:

The honey gains speed as it falls, so for the same volume flow rate, it
takes less cross-sectional dimension. You can demonstrate this with your
bathtub faucet. Water does the same thing, but at a different rate, because
it's less viscous.

• • •

Dear Marilyn:
Please explain the "straw effect." This is where you hold your finger over the end of a straw, and you can pick it up and hold liquid inside. Does it have to do with surface tension?

Pat Whiteman
Fort Worth, Texas

Dear Pat:
Surface tension and atmospheric pressure, actually. Try this for some fun. Put a piece of cardboard over the top of a glass of water. (Don't worry about filling it all the way.) Then, holding the cardboard firmly in place, turn the glass over and remove your hand. Surprise! The cardboard stays in place, and the water stays in the glass.

When you turn the glass over, the water starts to fall, leaving the air inside the glass at a lower pressure than the air outside it. This difference holds the water up, and even more force is added by the surface tension between the water and the cardboard.

• • •

Dear Marilyn:
You're given the two containers illustrated below. Filled with water, which of the two will have a greater underwater pressure?

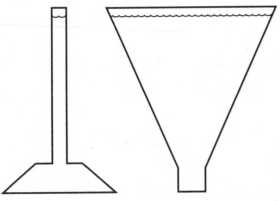

Robin Ireton
Mustang, Oklahoma

Dear Robin:
Surprisingly, the pressure will be equal. In a given liquid, pressure depends only on the depth and is independent of the size or shape of the container.

• • •

Dear Marilyn:
Let's say you're sitting in a boat in the middle of a pool, and you're holding a brick. You drop the brick over the side into the water. What happens to the water level of the pool? Does it go up, down, or remain the same?

J. R. Brosius
Lansford, Pennsylvania

Dear Reader:
As bricks are heavier than water, the level of the pool will go down. (Not that you're going to notice it all that much.) This is because the brick in the boat displaces water by weight, but the brick in the pool displaces water by volume. Let's suppose for a moment that a brick weighs two times as much as its equivalent volume of water. When it's floating, then, it would displace two bricks of water. But when it's lying on the bottom of the pool, it would displace only one brick of water. And when less water is displaced, the level drops.

• • •

Dear Marilyn:
A guide told our tour group in Hawaii that there was no such thing as a tidal wave! How could he possibly say this?

Joey Rappo
Grandview, Washington

Dear Joey:
Tides cause plenty of waves, all right, but they don't cause the blockbuster sort you're talking about. Those are caused by movement of the ocean floor, instead. More correctly called "tsunamis" (soo-NAH-meez), they're "seismic waves," not "tidal waves."

• • •

Dear Marilyn:
What is the true source of the sound we hear when we hold a seashell up to our ears? It isn't really the ocean, is it?

Irene Kruse
Brandon, Florida

Dear Irene:
No, but it's a cute myth, isn't it? Because of the shape of certain shells, they echo back many of the ordinary sounds occurring nearby, the combina-

tion of them all producing a sort of "white noise" that resembles the sound of surf.

•   •   •

Dear Marilyn:
Is there more water above the surface of the earth, including oceans, lakes, rivers, and so on, or is there more water below the surface of the earth?

Larry Breeden
Elizabeth, Colorado

Dear Larry:
Even going down more than two miles underground, we find less than 1 percent of the earth's water. If we pollute the surface water, we've had it.

•   •   •

Dear Marilyn:
Does the amount of water on the earth really stay the same?

Mariana Ross
Raleigh, North Carolina

Dear Mariana:
That's what scientists think. Despite changing percentages among things like glaciers versus the oceans versus the ice cubes in your tea, the total amount of water on Earth is thought to have remained constant. And as things haven't changed much over the last billion years, I don't think we need to run around and fill all the bathtubs anytime soon.

•   •   •

Dear Marilyn:
Environmentalists claim that plastic can last for thousands of years without biodegrading, and librarians worry that the world's books are literally rotting on their shelves. Why, then, can't books be printed on plastic paper? That way, not only would books last far longer than most of them are worth, but I could read while soaking in the tub without having to worry.

Paula Steiner
Lake Charles, Louisiana

Dear Paula:
The Library of Congress estimates that more than 25 percent of its books are brittle and possibly unusable, and another 50 percent are endangered. Although plastic processes already are used to preserve information, I don't

envision "permanent" books as the answer. Considering much of what I see in the bookstores these days, what environmentalist would want them around that long?

• • •

Dear Marilyn:

When you put two dozen navy beans into a jar with hundreds of kidney beans and shake them a few times, the beans are pretty well distributed. But the navy beans won't come back together, no matter how much you shake the jar. Likewise, you can add chocolate syrup to a glass of milk, and it makes chocolate milk with a little stirring. But the chocolate will never come back together, regardless of how many times you stir it. What is the law that produces this activity?

> Leon Vogel
> Murrietta, California

Dear Leon:

It's called "entropy," the scientific term for the natural tendency of systems to move toward greater "disorder" as time passes. For example, once you've scrambled an egg, the yolk and albumen won't naturally separate and gather back together again in the eggshell. The term also applies to the thermodynamics (heat-transfer properties) of the universe as a whole and is the reason some physicists say that all of our useful energy might someday be so evenly dispersed that life (and even motion) would no longer be possible. It's difficult to reconcile this principle with birth and evolution and the rise of civilization—after all, chickens will continue to lay more eggs—but it's not impossible, at least for those in the field of thermodynamics.

• • •

Dear Marilyn:

Why is it that when the space shuttle blasts off, Mission Control says, "Engines operating at 104 percent"? I always thought that 100 percent was the most you get out of *anything*.

> Michael Lindner
> Ann Arbor, Michigan

Dear Michael:

Well, trust NASA to do even better than that. They've improved upon the original design point of the shuttle, and it's now capable of more thrust. Actually, it can operate at up to 109 percent of its earlier-rated power at sea level (which was only an estimate, anyway). But 104 percent is the limit of current use, which the shuttle can achieve as it climbs in altitude and into a less-dense atmosphere.

• • •

Dear Marilyn:
On the first television shot of the *Challenger* blowing up, there was a little parachute that came out of the explosion on the righthand side. The next time they showed the film, the parachute was cut out, and I must have seen it that way twenty-five times that day. Then late one night, I saw the parachute again. Why hasn't anyone explained this to us? Has it been hushed up by the government for some reason?

H. L. Hawk
Shamokin, Pennsylvania

Dear Reader:
You certainly have a sharp eye, but plenty of people were there to witness the *Challenger* disaster in person, so it wouldn't be possible for anything to be hidden. NASA completed an investigation of the parachute sighting, and here's what happened: In a successful launch, the two external rockets separate from the ship and return via parachutes to be used again. However, in the *Challenger* launch, there was an explosion seventy-three seconds after takeoff. Three seconds later, a rocket booster nosecap separated, deploying the chute that would have opened more normally in better circumstances.

• • •

Dear Marilyn:
If you're at the north magnetic pole, which way will your compass point?

Jared Fritz
Ephrata, Pennsylvania

Dear Jared:
If you allow your compass needle to follow any angle, it will point *downward*.

• • •

Dear Marilyn:
I have asked many engineers this question and have yet to receive an answer, which I don't know myself. You are given two identical rectangular iron blocks. One of the blocks is a magnet, the other is not. The blocks are

now placed on a wooden table. Using only the two blocks and nothing else, you are asked to determine which one is which. Can this be done?

Jerry Audler
Metairie, Louisiana

Dear Jerry:

Yes, and this is a good one for science classes. Take two iron rods, one magnetized and one not. Pick up one rod and carefully touch either end of it to the middle of the other rod. If the rods stick together, the one you're holding is the magnet. If they don't, the one lying on the table is the magnet.

But why? If the one you picked up is the magnet, either end of it will be attracted to anywhere along the whole length of the one on the table. But if the one on the table is the magnet instead, the one you picked up will touch it right where it's weakest—midway between its two poles.

● ● ●

Dear Marilyn:

Every time I exit my car, I'm zapped by the next object I touch. Just how much voltage is in that spark jumping from the end of my finger?

Don Wood
Dunn, North Carolina

Dear Don:

In that situation, you might be left fifteen thousand volts higher than ground potential. Although the accompanying amps are so low that you don't feel much more than a sting, this is why static electricity can be so destructive to the delicate microcircuitry used in sophisticated computers. Shocking, isn't it?!

● ● ●

Dear Marilyn:

My car has fabric seats. Every time I get out of it, I get a static electric shock when I touch the door. How can I avoid getting shocked?

Richard Rockwell
Malvern, Pennsylvania

Dear Richard:

Just use your car key to touch the next effectively grounded, conducting object, like the car door.

● ● ●

Dear Marilyn:
   After I bumped my head into a high-speed ceiling fan, I told someone that the extremities of the blades traveled at a higher speed than at the source of power. However, this person claimed that the same RPM existed at both points. Who is right?

Ken Rouse
Venice, Florida

Dear Ken:
   You both are. Revolutions per minute and speed are two different concepts. Think of racehorses circling a track. If they stay in their post position lanes all the way around to a finish line set where they began, the outside horse, who has to travel a greater distance than the inside horse, must run much faster to keep up. But they've both run just one revolution.

● ● ●

Dear Marilyn:
   Here in the desert, everyone wants to keep cool. If ceiling fans have the same size motor and blades, which one will produce the most movement of air—a fan with two, three, four, or five blades?

William Trush
Tempe, Arizona

Dear William:
   The number of blades is only one of many factors that affect air movement. Shape is another. For example, let's say that fan A and fan B are identical, except that A has three blades and B has four. With one type of blade, A may have more air movement, but with another shape blade, B may have more. If this weren't the case, all windmills would look like Japanese fans.

● ● ●

Dear Marilyn:
   I recently installed a large mirror, and several lamps are now reflected in it. My room seems much lighter. Is this possible? Does the light reflect back into the room?

Violet Walker
Salt Lake City, Utah

Dear Violet:
   It certainly does, and with modern manufacturing techniques, this means you now easily achieve right there in your apartment what Louis XIV had

to try so hard to accomplish in his mirror gallery at Versailles! A smooth mirrored surface may reflect more than 90 percent of the visible light. A white wall still reflects some 80 percent of it, but as the surface is rough by comparison, it returns the light much more diffusely. A black wall, on the other hand, typically reflects less than 10 percent of visible light.

Thirteen

Dear Marilyn:
  Why don't people in the Southern Hemisphere feel horizontal or upside down? This question has puzzled me for many years.
                                                                Mark Novak
                                                                Staten Island, New York

Dear Mark:
  For the same reason we don't. We're physically oriented by gravity, not by map direction, and we're psychologically oriented by map direction, not by gravity. The most important thing to note, however, is that while gravity is very real, map direction is entirely arbitrary. Putting north on the top all the time is a convenience, not a necessity. It would be just as valid to put *south* on the top.

● ● ●

Dear Marilyn:
  When appliances like a television and calculator are shut off, a series of eights appear. Is there a reason why that number eight is chosen? Why not another number?
                                                                Diane Podrasky
                                                                Johnstown, Pennsylvania

Dear Diane:
  Turn on your calculator and enter the number "8." See the lines (probably seven) of which it's composed? Those are the same lines that make all the other digits. (Try entering a row of them, and you'll see how it's done.) And when every one of those lines is displayed at the same time, the pattern that results, by coincidence, looks exactly like the numeral "8."

• • •

Dear Marilyn:

What is the reason broken appliances suddenly begin working as soon as you demonstrate the problem to a service technician?

Phil Milstein
Cambridge, Massachusetts

Dear Phil:

For the same reason that people occasionally sit up in the morgue. They may not be in such good shape, but they're not quite dead yet, either.

• • •

Dear Marilyn:

If aeronautical engineers can make indestructible "black boxes" that can survive airplane crashes, then why don't they just make entire airplanes out of the material of which the black boxes are made?

Janet Gribnitz
Dallas, Texas

Dear Janet:

Who cares about the plane? The trick is to make *people* out of the stuff.

• • •

Dear Marilyn:

We've been driving cars since the turn of the century, and we've been wearing out tires by the millions. Where does all the rubber go? It's not in the streets or roadsides, and it's not in the air. (No one ever complains about "rubber pollution.")

William Lavers
West Palm Beach, Florida

Dear William:

No place special. Nearly all of it simply settles as dust along the roadways. But why such interest in tires? We've been wearing out shoes for a lot longer, and no one seems to care where our soles go. (And please, folks. Don't send me any puns about that last line, okay?)

• • •

Dear Marilyn:

I'd like to know why it is that when driving up a hill, it doesn't look so steep, but when you drive back down the same hill, it looks much steeper.

D. Reitz
Summerville, Pennsylvania

Dear Reader:
Gravity may be the answer—the fear of your brakes failing. (Try walking next time. I'll bet it'll look steeper on the way *up*!)

• • •

Dear Marilyn:
In movies and on television programs, one sees the letters "E C N A L U B M A" on the front of ambulances. Why is it spelled backwards? Does it serve a purpose?

Frank Lawrence
Syracuse, New York

Dear Frank:
Have another look at it next time. The word is *reversed*, not spelled backward, and it's that way in real life as well as in the movies. This is to make it easier for you (while driving a vehicle) to read the word "AMBULANCE" on the vehicle behind you (and thus realize you should get out of the way) when you look in one of your rear-view mirrors to see what all the commotion back there is about.

• • •

Dear Marilyn:
But why isn't the driver of the ambulance also reversed? (From the left front seat to the right front seat.)

Robert Reardon
Leesburg, Florida

Dear Robert:
Oh, but the driver *is* reversed. Turn around and look directly at the ambulance. The driver is on your right. Now look in the rear-view mirror. The driver is on your left.

• • •

Dear Marilyn:
What would be the cost for an average car without all the advertising we pay for?

G. J. Mundle
Stratford, Connecticut

Dear Reader:
The proportion that goes to publicity and promotion isn't really as much as we might think from hearing all those huge annual figures. For example,

in 1990, General Motors spent about 1.5 percent of their total sales income on the media. If that were applicable to every automobile they manufactured, it would mean that on a twenty-thousand-dollar car, only three hundred dollars was spent on advertising.

•   •   •

Dear Marilyn:

This is the result of a game that we and our friends played, and we've all agreed to bow to your decision. Can a bassinet be considered a vehicle? Our dictionary defines a vehicle as any device for carrying persons or objects, and my wife and I have transported our newborn son in a bassinet from place to place. In that context, I contend that the bassinet is a "vehicle." What do you think?

J. R. Gibbs
Sheffield, Alabama

Dear Reader:

I think you've gone a wee bit too far on this one. By *your* standards, until just recently, your *wife* was a vehicle.

•   •   •

Dear Marilyn:

Why don't we just leave the geographical subdivisions out of the address on our domestic mail? The ZIP code alone is sufficient and more precise than the city and state, and we would save the time and effort in writing the address.

Milton Ragsdale
Austin, Texas

Dear Milton:

How nice to hear from the picturesque town of 78731. The ZIP code is certainly more precise than the city and state—especially the new nine-digit codes that can pinpoint a city block or even a single floor of an office building. However, using *only* the ZIP code might actually slow the entire mail system because of the number of errors made. The U.S. Postal Service informs us that 3.14 percent of first-class mail has the wrong ZIP code, and without the city and state as a cross-check, all those letters and packages would have to go back to the sender.

•   •   •

Dear Marilyn:

Why is it you can tear a newspaper up and down straight, but you can't tear it straight across?

Stanley Cohen
Palm Coast, Florida

Dear Stanley:
For the most part, newsprint is made with a vertical grain in order to run the presses without tearing it. If it were really important for readers to be able to rip out articles more neatly, that could be accomplished, but the price of the newspaper would soar. (And scissors do a better job, anyway.)

• • •

Dear Marilyn:
Could you please tell me how decaffeinated coffee is made? I'm really concerned about some of the things I've heard.
Marge Spair
Robbinsville, New Jersey

Dear Marge:
The most prevalent method uses water and carbon dioxide to extract the caffeine from green coffee before roasting. Chemical solvents may also be used, but they're regulated by the Food and Drug Administration.
And you might be interested to know that this caffeine isn't wasted. Much of it is sold to the pharmaceutical industry for use in various drugs, including diet pills and headache remedies. But that's not all. (Are you sitting down, Marge?) The caffeine also is sold to the soft-drink industry! Cola drinks contain so little caffeine naturally that cola companies strengthen it themselves, adding nearly *ten times* as much caffeine to give it the punch that people have come to expect.

• • •

Dear Marilyn:
Are there alternatives to producing food instead of the time-consuming process of planting and harvesting? Can we mix chemicals together to make food?
Suzie Pestrock
Reading, Pennsylvania

Dear Suzie:
We're trying. Something appetizing called SCP (single-cell protein) can be produced without agriculture. Other possible yummies include lysine, methionine, tryptophan, and threonine. Just think! Someday we might sit down to dinner at our favorite restaurant and find ourselves saying, "Hey, I think I'd like a bowl of 1,3-butanediol for an appetizer, and what would you recommend for the main course? Any nice fatty acids tonight? Fine, I'll try the 2,4-dimethylheptanoic."

• • •

Dear Marilyn:
I've seen pecans, walnuts, almonds, and filberts in the shell. Why have I never seen cashews in the shell?

Eleanor Blumberg
Hollywood, Florida

Dear Eleanor:
Because they wouldn't be much fun to get *out* of that shell. The cashew shell has two walls, with a blackish oil between them that can blister human skin and is sometimes used as an insecticide. Even roasting the shells open gives off injurious fumes, unless it's done by an expert. What an unwelcome addition to your bowl of unshelled nuts!

• • •

Dear Marilyn:
What is sodium erythorbate? It's found in bologna and other lunchmeats, and I've been told that it's a preservative made from earthworms. Is that the truth?

Mrs. Willie Jackson
Nampa, Idaho

Dear Reader:
Only half of it is true. Yes, sodium erythorbate is a preservative, but no, it isn't made from earthworms. And if that's a disappointment to any younger folks reading this who were secretly hoping to discover something really yucky, has anyone heard of the National Earthworm Cooking Contest? (No, I didn't really think you had.) Yes, there was such a thing, but the last I heard of it was back in the late seventies, and it doesn't surprise me that it didn't turn into an annual event.

• • •

Dear Marilyn:
You can't trust what you buy any more. Since when did "ice cream" come to mean anything from frozen yogurt to a big glob of processed seaweed?

Arnold Fulsome
Suncook, New Hampshire

Dear Arnold:
It happened about the time that "red" became a flavor instead of a color. I can often be found at a nearby snowcone stand on a warm day, asking for "one green, please."

• • •

Dear Marilyn:
My great-granddaughter has come up with a good question. Why does the Easter Bunny deliver eggs when it's a *chicken* that lays eggs?

Jeanette Meier
El Cajon, California

Dear Jeanette:
Let's not talk about this in print, Jeanette. The situation is silly enough already; we don't want to start an Easter Chicken, do we?

• • •

Dear Marilyn:
This question is very important to me and my family. I'm seventy-two, and all my life, when I eat corn on the cob, whether roasted or boiled, when I get through, the cob is exactly square. I have no intent to do this. It doesn't matter if the ear is big or small, mature or less so. No one else I know has this happen. When we eat out, same thing. I have half-a-dozen degrees, including two doctorates, and I have written to the philosophy and psychology departments of my universities to ask about the significance of this, and they are as baffled as I am.

Bob Hunter
Thomasville, Georgia

Dear Bob:
You sure wrote to the right two departments! The philosophy people can discuss whether the cob is actually square, and the other people can discuss *you*. But maybe we can just see you as an ongoing experiment. (Everyone who takes Bob Hunter out to dinner should make sure to get him an ear of corn and observe how the cob is *always square* afterward.) And be sure to invite the grandkids to dinner more often. Why, someone might discover a new law of physics right there in your mouth!

As good as I've become at predicting which questions will draw a huge response, there are still plenty that come as a complete surprise, and that last question was one of them. The following column was the result.

Dear Marilyn:
I'd like to comment on the letter from Bob Hunter, who wanted to know why his corn cob was square after he finished eating. In order for the cob

to remain round, he'd have to wrap his mouth around it and drag his teeth across the surface.

> Stephen Griffis
> McGraw, New York

After a family dinner, mine was the only round cob—the others were square. We concluded that they use the typewriter method, while I use the lathe method.

> Susan Treff
> Baltimore, Maryland

A slight overbite will account for the squareness. I ate corn on the cob last night with my parents. Mom's was round, Dad's was disgusting, and mine was square. I considered bronzing it to send to you or Bob.

> Kimberle Byrd
> Wyoming, Michigan

My cobs are square, too. I think it means that we're thorough eaters—we clean the cob to the core, which *is* square.

> Penny Dickerson
> Beaver Dam, Utah

Every corn cob I have ever seen is round. Tell Bob to go to any grain elevator and look. They're round.

> Alice Chittenden
> Spring Lake, Michigan

Tell Bob Hunter from Georgia that my wife, also from Georgia, and all our children and grandchildren also finish off with square cobs—except for a grandchild, who often finishes off with a triangle cob. I think it must be genetic. Ask Mr. Hunter if his grandfather was named George.

> Morris Katz
> Stanley, Virginia

I have a five-year-old springer spaniel that does exactly the same thing.

> John Campbell
> Phoenix, Arizona

Please advise 72-year-old Bob Hunter that if he is still eating corn on the cob at his age, he is way ahead of the game.

> Bernard Reis
> Maplewood, New Jersey

Dear Readers:

Hmmm. I'm still thinking about the kid who ends up with the triangular cobs. But in the meantime, I think the following reader deserves to have the last word.

Dear Marilyn:

As a specialist working in the area of human factors, I would suggest that Mr. Hunter is a member of one of the more elite groups of corn-on-the-cob eaters. The attached diagram illustrates what most probably occurs when Mr. Hunter is processing an ear of corn.

Walter Talley
Pennsville, New Jersey

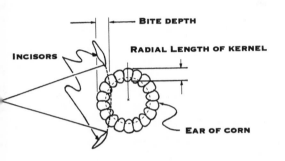

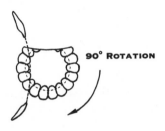

STEP 1- Initial series of Bites.

STEP 2- First Rotation, second series of Bites.

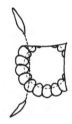

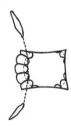

STEP 3 - Second Rotation, third series of Bites

STEP 4 - Third Rotation, final series of Bites.

FINAL PRODUCT- A "square" cob.

Dear Readers:

These days, there's a specialist in *everything!*

Fourteen

Dear Marilyn:

As a theologian, I've always been fascinated by the Bible's account of the awe-inspiring sign of the rainbow. What has baffled me is why one never sees more than one rainbow at a time. Do you know the reason?

Rabbi Arnold Stiebel
Fort Worth, Texas

Dear Rabbi Stiebel:

For starters, rainbows must always appear opposite the sun, but the next time you see one, remember Dorothy in *The Wizard of Oz* and look somewhere *over* the rainbow. There are often two of them: a bright bow (with red on the outside and violet on the inside) and a larger, dim one (with red on the inside and violet on the outside).

What a dazzling (and unexpected) response we received to that last question. Readers everywhere sent me their double-rainbow photos, and my bulletin board became very colorful indeed. And after this next question, the office brightened all over again—this time with the compliments of pilots and other frequent flyers.

Dear Marilyn:

I saw a rainbow—not a half-circle, but a whole circle. According to the flight logbook for that date, we were between Tallahassee and Cedar Key, Florida, at approximately eighteen-hundred feet, traveling north to south about two miles offshore, and there were clouds and storm cells everywhere. Is this unusual?

Kerry Mathews
Port Charlotte, Florida

Dear Kerry:
It's unusual to witness, but not to occur. Whole rainbows occasionally are seen from planes because they're not cut off by the horizon. (But I wish I could have been there.)

• • •

Dear Marilyn:
After years of trying, I finally saw the "green flash." Can you tell me more about it? Is it an optical illusion?

Ray Wilbert
Vista, California

Dear Ray:
I'm envious. I've never seen the green flash myself and have even wondered if it existed—despite the fact that it has been well documented, especially by explorers at the South Pole. I don't know much about it, but the flash occurs just as the top of the sun sets beneath (or rises above) a flat, clear horizon, and it's probably caused by the separation of the sunlight's colors by the atmosphere.
I hope you don't have to wait years for the next one.

Quite a few people wrote to suggest that the "green flash" is simply nature's way of relieving the eye fatigue caused by lengthy exposure to a particular color and that gazing at anything red for long enough eventually will cause the complementary color of green to appear. One person even enclosed a red felt disk for me to use as an experiment, and it worked very well.

But there's more to the "green flash" than that. And after reading articles in Scientific American, The Smithsonian, *and other magazines, I'm quite confident that it's a very real atmospheric phenomenon.*

• • •

Dear Marilyn:
Is there such a thing as a "blue moon"?

Ginny Gamache
Rosemead, California

Dear Ginny:
Yes, but as you might have suspected, it occurs very rarely. (This is where we get the expression, "once in a blue moon.") When there are enough dust particles of a particular size in the air that scatter more light at the red end of the color spectrum than at the blue end, the red light "disappears"

into the night sky, and the moon shining through the unscattered light looks blue.

• • •

Dear Marilyn:
   At a NASA presentation, I asked the team why no pictures taken in space show stars. The background behind the subject is uniformly black. They didn't know, but the astronauts themselves described "millions of stars all around." So why can't we see them?

                                                            John Quinn
                                                            Tulelake, California

Dear John:
   The limitation of photography is the answer. If you focus on the Earth, the required film, shutter speed, and lens aperture will not record the (relatively) fainter light of the stars. But if you turn away and focus only on the stars themselves, using a different film, speed, and aperture, you can photograph them in all their glory.

• • •

Dear Marilyn:
   Why is the North Star always in the same sighting in the northern heavens?
                                                            D. M. Brock
                                                            Bloomington, Indiana

Dear Reader:
   Because the Earth's north rotational axis very nearly points to it. This makes the North Star seem stationary, but it isn't, really. The unaided eye just can't detect that small a circle of apparent movement. In addition, Polaris was not always the North Star and, in true Hollywood fashion, will move on at some point in the future to be replaced by another.

• • •

Dear Marilyn:
   When looking at a star flash, am I seeing a flash that occurred thousands of light-years ago due to the time it takes light to travel in a year, or am I seeing it as it occurs?

                                                            Brent Myers
                                                            Yakima, Washington

Dear Brent:
   When you look at the stars, you're looking deeply into the past. It makes you wonder what's out there *right now*, doesn't it?

• • •

Dear Marilyn:
   If it takes millions of years for light to travel to Earth from some of the planets, how do we know whether they all still even exist?
                              J. W. Clifford
                              Denver, Colorado

Dear Reader:
   Compared to the stars, the planets are in our backyard. Even Pluto, the ninth planet and the one farthest away (most of the time), averages only 3,664,000,000 ordinary miles away from the sun. If the speed of light is around 186,282 miles per second, light reflected from Pluto would reach us in about five and a half hours. So if a scientist sees the planet through a telescope after dinner, he or she can rest assured that Pluto was at least still there at lunch.

• • •

Dear Marilyn:
   Back when I was in grade school, we were taught a sentence to help us memorize the planets, but I've forgotten it over the years. It went something like, "Martha Visits Mary Every Sunday Just . . ." Do you know how it goes?
                              Mrs. K. E. Johnson
                              Olympia, Washington

Dear Reader:
   Sounds like that sentence could use updating. (And that a couple of planets may have slipped out of place!) How about this one of my own? In addition to the names of the planets, it also fixes their order in average distance from the sun. "Mankind's Verdant Earth Must Journey (as a) Star Unites Nine Planets." (And if you don't readily remember which "M" planet goes with which "M" word, keep in mind that "mankind" has the same number of letters as Mercury, and "must" has the same number of letters as Mars.)

PLANET NO. 1	Mercury	Mankind's
PLANET NO. 2	Venus	Verdant
PLANET NO. 3	Earth	Earth
PLANET NO. 4	Mars	Must
PLANET NO. 5	Jupiter	Journey (as a)
PLANET NO. 6	Saturn	Star
PLANET NO. 7	Uranus	Unites
PLANET NO. 8	Neptune	Nine
PLANET NO. 9	Pluto	Planets

● ● ●

Dear Marilyn:

Why don't we dump toxic waste and nonbiodegradable garbage into outer space?

Barbara Webb
West Columbia, South Carolina

Dear Barbara:

Oh, please! We should have learned by now from our experience with polluted oceans and atmospheres that you can't throw anything "away." There's even garbage orbiting the earth. In addition to the more than one thousand satellites out there, there are tens of thousands of pieces of debris, ranging from whole junked rocket stages to nuts and bolts, revolving like a trashy asteroid belt around the planet.

In a way, it sounds almost naïve to imagine that our inconceivably vast cosmos could ever be contaminated, but there was a time when people couldn't imagine that a vast ocean could ever be contaminated, either. And even if we managed to pollute "only" our own little corner of the world, leaving the rest of the cosmos pristine, would that be acceptable?

● ● ●

Dear Marilyn:

We would send a mouse into space, not an elephant. So why do we send six-foot, 250-pound male astronauts into space when five-foot, 100-pound female astronauts could do the same job?

Phill Bohan
Quincy, Massachusetts

Dear Phill:

Well, what if one of the windows would get stuck shut?

Fifteen

Dear Marilyn:
Why do archaeologists have to dig to find artifacts? Does everything sink into the earth?

Mary Romero
New Iberia, Louisiana

Dear Mary:
Very little actually sinks. Instead, artifacts first get covered and then buried, and by many forces—both civilized and uncivilized. There are dust and dirt (and the resultant plants), and ash and sand, and water and ice (such as creeping glaciers), and there are earthquakes and volcanoes, too. And then there are people, who build on top of other things rather than tear them back down to ground zero. And how deep is ground zero, anyway? How would you like to start to build a house and be told you need to dig back down to the end of the Pleistocene Age?

•   •   •

Dear Marilyn:
In a discussion among friends, we were unable to figure out how 1994 could be in the twentieth century. For example, a child born in the year A.D. 1 would have to have been born in the zero century, because the first century would not have occurred for another ninety-nine years. Can you explain?

Hughe's Lounge
Roseland, Louisiana

Dear Readers:
That child would have been born in the first century, you guys. Look at it this way: If you were born on a Wednesday morning, would you say you were born on a nameless day because Wednesday hadn't finished yet?!

• • •

Dear Marilyn:

Why does the International Date Line follow such a crazy route? Why isn't it a straight north-south line?

Richard Zollweg
Laguna Beach, California

Dear Richard:

For the same reason that the dividing lines around time zones aren't always straight up and down. It makes life more difficult for people when boundaries go right through cities or states or other important political entities (like your dining-room table) unnecessarily, so the lines deviate around them as much as possible. And there's no significant loss in precision. Creating time zones one hour in width is completely arbitrary, so the places that have the most accurate time are in the *middle* of the zones, anyway. In other words, people close to opposite sides of the same boundary aren't really an hour apart in time. *Minutes* is more like it.

• • •

Dear Marilyn:

Many of us wonder why the law is on the books that switches the time clock backward in the fall. For what purpose did it start? Any advantages must be overwhelmed by the disadvantages. Accidents occur more frequently, and fuel bills go up. I have talked to many people over the years, and no one wants it.

Fritz Parker
San Diego, California

Dear Fritz:

Maybe you haven't talked with enough people! In 1986, when the most recent Daylight Saving Time legislation was signed in, the Department of Transportation estimated that just moving up the start of summer time from the last Sunday in April to the first Sunday *alone* would save $28 million in automobile accidents and prevent fifteen hundred injuries and twenty deaths. However, the original reason for the time change was to conserve fuel, and Benjamin Franklin was among the earlier advocates who hoped to save many candles this way.

But maybe this is all beside the point. If the law were removed, it would *not* prevent the winter situation you describe. Daylight Saving Time is what moves the clock forward in the spring. *Stopping* it is what moves the clock backward again in the fall. In other words, it's the *regular* time you don't like!

•   •   •

Dear Marilyn:
Why do clocks start with twelve at the top instead of one?
Ron Hoover
South Bend, Indiana

Dear Ron:
For the same reason that scales do. Just as the round dial on a scale begins with zero and progresses on through a given number of divisions on its way to a pound, the day begins at midnight and progresses on through an hour on its way to one o'clock. That is, the clock can be seen as a kind of scale that weighs twelve hours; envisioning a zero above the twelve might help.

•   •   •

Dear Marilyn:
What time is it (to the second) when both the hour and minute hands on a clock are precisely overlapping on (almost on, that is) the number six?
Louis Eisen
Oceanside, California

Dear Louis:
Perhaps the time you're looking for is 6:32.727272 (etc.) But did you know that there are *two* such times, each equidistant from the number six? The other is 5:27.272727 (etc.).

•   •   •

Dear Marilyn:
How often does the minute hand on a clock pass the hour hand between noon and midnight?
Samuel Lloyd
Frederica, Delaware

Dear Samuel:
Odd, isn't it? It's only ten times (unless you count both noon and midnight).

This one drove people crazy, too. Here's a sampling of the mail that followed:

Dear Marilyn:

I'm surprised you didn't think twice about your answer to the question, "How often does the minute hand on a clock pass the hour hand between noon and midnight?"—unless you're trying to see how many people read your column. You answered "ten times (not counting noon and midnight)." It should have been eleven times: No. 1 at 1:05, No. 2 at 2:10, No. 3 at 3:15, No. 4 at 4:20, No. 5 at 5:25, No. 6 at 6:30, No. 7 at 7:35, No. 8 at 8:40, No. 9 at 9:45, No. 10 at 10:50, and No. 11 at 11:55.

> R. J. Willeke
> Grandview, Missouri

Your clock must have stopped when you said that. If you have any doubts, use your fingers to count the hours starting with one o'clock and finishing with eleven o'clock.

> Milton Kee
> Memphis, Tennessee

Shame on you for your casual answer. Your response was incorrect, but even you are allowed the luxury of error on occasion. There's only been one perfect person in the history of mankind, and they crucified him!

> Donald Jordan
> Nantucket, Massachusetts

It's eleven times, not ten—but I don't expect a reply as I'm sure you're too embarrassed at being proved wrong by a man.

> Edward Lee
> Billings, Montana

It's *eleven* times. 11! Boy, are you gonna get it.

> William Sommerwerck
> Bellevue, Washington

But the original answer is indeed correct. The answer of eleven times (sent by the readers above) are wrong—the two hands can cross only ten *times (not including noon and midnight), as follows:*

# 1 at 1:05.454545	# 6 at 6:32.727272
# 2 at 2:10.909090	# 7 at 7:38.181818
# 3 at 3:16.363636	# 8 at 8:43.636363
# 4 at 4:21.818181	# 9 at 9:49.090909
# 5 at 5:27.272727	#10 at 10:54.545454.

To convince themselves of this, the readers who wrote in can take an old-fashioned watch or clock, start at 12:00 and wind the minute hand through the hours themselves. They'll see, for example, that at the 11:55 time mentioned by one of them, the minute hand is on the eleven, but the hour hand is nearly on the twelve. (And the address to which to write with further protestations is at the end of this book!)

Part Three

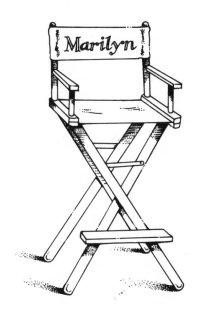

Sixteen

THINKING

ANALYTICALLY

Dear Marilyn:

I've frequently wondered if you derive an equation for the math problems sent to you, or do you just work out the numbers until they fit? If you do derive an equation, could you include it with your answer for those of us with an interest in math?

Ellen Henderson
Clearwater, Florida

Dear Ellen:

We often explain an answer as fully as we have room, but we don't usually provide the formula because I personally feels it shuts off the thinking process as much as the enjoyment. Reasons make far better teachers, and this is a fun-and-profit column, after all. Who wants to lean back and open the Sunday paper to find equations lurking in there?! As for me, I'd enjoy it about as much as finding barracuda in my bathtub.

Here's a nice excerpt from a letter I received from a graduate student in math after one of my many "word" solutions.

Dear Marilyn:

In a recent column, you were asked for a mathematical solution to a problem. You gave a nice solution using mathematical logic with no mathematical symbols.

To have given the solution using equations—something I know you could have done—would have taken up all the space in your column and would have encouraged many readers to turn the page. . . .

Michael Rosenborg
San Luis Obispo, California

Hmmm. It occurs to me that in a book, the author wants *the reader to turn the page!*

• • •

Dear Marilyn:

Here's mathematical proof that two equals one:

If $A = B$, and you multiply both sides by A, you get $A^2 = AB$. If you subtract B^2 from both sides, you get $A^2 - B^2 = AB - B^2$. Factoring both sides makes it $(A + B)(A - B) = B(A - B)$. Then dividing both sides by $(A - B)$ leaves $A + B = B$. And knowing that $A = B$, this means that $B + B = B$, or $2B = B$, or $2 = 1$.

How come?

> David Turner
> Arlington, Texas

Dear David:

See where you divided both sides by $(A - B)$? Well, because A and B are equal, A minus B equals zero, and you can't divide by zero. At least not without the above bizarre consequence!

• • •

Dear Marilyn:

I'm in grade school, and we're studying how to multiply decimals. I do it well, but I don't understand why the answer is the way it is. How can you multiply something and have it get *smaller*? I asked my math teacher, but I didn't understand her explanation, so she told me to write and ask you.

> Brandy Elrod
> Pendergrass, Georgia

Dear Brandy:

Do you know how we say "times" when we multiply? It means "occurrences," as in the sentence, "I went skating yesterday and fell two times." Try substituting that word in your equation. "Two times three" can be translated as "two occurrences of a group of three." (Which equals six.) When we translate ".5 times three" to "half an occurrence of three," it's a little easier to see why the result will be less. (Or only 1½.) "Half an occurrence" is clearly smaller than the whole occurrence.

• • •

Dear Marilyn:

I'm in college and pursuing a degree in aerospace engineering, but I'm having enormous difficulty with the following class: physics with calculus.

SAFETY IN NUMBERS   113

Why do I struggle so much with physics when I am very talented at advanced mathematics, such as linear algebra, coding theory, and complex analysis? I went into this class thinking it would be a breeze, but I've fallen flat on my face, and I'm at a loss to explain why.

Kevin Dore
Jupiter, Florida

Dear Kevin:

This is only a guess, of course, but mathematics is an extremely exact science, and although physics would be if it could, it must operate on a fair amount of faith at present. Whole bodies of thought rest uneasily on theories that have never been proven, some of which will someday be found to be totally wrong. Then again, you could be generalizing prematurely. Maybe your instructor just isn't good for you.

● ● ●

Dear Marilyn:

I'm not an advocate of fast driving, but I'm puzzled by the notion that driving more slowly saves gas. If I have fifty miles to drive and keep the speed limit of 55 mph, wouldn't it take me longer to get there—and therefore make me burn *more* gas—than if I had driven faster and gotten there more quickly?

Reverend Kevin Shanley
Darien, Illinois

Dear Reverend Shanley:

No. Although you spend a little more time on the road, the fuel that you use in that time is less than the extra fuel you would have used to travel at a higher speed. (Now, that doesn't even look clear to *me*, and I *wrote* it!) Whether you get there fast, slow, or somewhere in the middle, when you *do* get there, you will have used less gas. And if gas, not time, is your consideration, you will be ahead. (Theoretically, anyway. In real life, it can depend on how your carburetor behaves.)

● ● ●

Dear Marilyn:

May I have your opinion on this? I received a speeding ticket. Two weeks later, my husband got stopped for driving 78 mph in a 65 mph zone. I told him that he should not have yelled at me for driving 52 mph in a 40 mph zone. He insists that if I knew my percentages, I would realize that my offense was greater than his. I still say that he simply drove one more mile over the speed limit than I did. (P.S. He also talked himself out of the speeding ticket.)

Rose Hieronymus
Brockton, Massachusetts

Dear Rose:

I think your husband's offense was worse. It's true that he drove only 1.2 times as fast as he should have, and you drove 1.3 times as fast, but why should that be the criterion? According to your husband's reasoning, driving 2 mph in a 1 mph zone (twice as fast as you should) is worse than driving 129 mph in a 65 mph zone (less than twice as fast as you should)! (P.S. And I think *both* of you should have yelled at the other.)

But plenty of people disagreed with me.

Dear Marilyn:

I disagree. The woman's offense is worse. The lower speed limit is there because conditions warrant it. Forty miles per hour is a residential speed limit where you may have more pedestrians around, while 65 mph is usually reserved for highways.

Craig Whitehead
Tallevast, Florida

Hers is a much worse offense because she had more chance of striking a pedestrian or another car than she would on the highway. Also, an accident at 78 mph is not much worse than one at 65 mph, but an accident at 52 mph *is* worse than one at 40 mph. Math has nothing to do with it.

Clarence Barnes, Jr.
Dallas, Texas

Dear Readers:

Math is very relevant here, but physics (an example of "math in action") has even more to do with it. For a car with a mass of "m" traveling at a speed of "v," the kinetic energy (the energy of motion) is $mv^2 \div 2$. This is a technical way of saying that the danger of high speeds is even greater than we might think. If the cars were alike, the wife's car had a multiple of 1352 energy units, but the husband's car had a multiple of 3042 energy units—more than twice as much. That is, an automobile traveling at 40 mph isn't just twice as hard to stop as one traveling at 20 mph. It's *four times* as hard to stop.

• • •

Dear Marilyn:
My mother and my two aunts went on a trip. They drove one aunt's car, which she had filled with gas. (My aunt didn't want to be paid for the use of her car.) The three of them each put $20 in a hat for gas for the trip. When they returned, they filled the car up. They had $27 left in the hat afterward. How do they split up the $27? Some say equally, and some say that since my aunt furnished the whole tank of gas before they left and also paid for one-third of the tank that is in the car now, she deserves more than one-third of the $27. Can you settle this?

Janet Aide
Highland, Wisconsin

Dear Janet:
They should split the money equally. Let's suppose *you* had lent your mother and aunts a car filled with gas. They took a trip, then returned your car with a full tank. Would you feel entitled to anything more? That's your aunt's position.

• • •

Dear Marilyn:
Say you deposit $50 in the bank. You write a check for $20, which leaves you $30. Then you write a check for $15, which leaves you $15. Then you write a check for $9, which leaves you $6. Then you write a check for $6, which leaves you nothing.

You deposit		$50.
Less a check for $20 equals		$30
Less a check for 15 equals		15
Less a check for 9 equals		6
Less a check for 6 equals		0
Totaling	$50	$51

Can you please explain why, after adding up what you had left, you come up with $1 more?

Karen Kinley
Whitesburg, Tennessee

Dear Karen:
What does the sum of the balances have to do with anything? In this case, they mislead because they happen to add up to just a dollar more than what was withdrawn. But suppose your transactions looked like this, instead.

You deposit $50.
Less a check for $1 equals $49
Less a check for 1 equals   48
Less a check for 1 equals   47
Less a check for 1 equals   46
Totaling $4 $190

We've only withdrawn $4 so far, and the sum of the balances is already *far* more than that. And that's probably why the sum doesn't look like anything special. It isn't!

• • •

Dear Marilyn:

A bank I dealt with sold me 20 checks for $1 for quite a while, which came to 5¢ a check. Later, they changed the price to 10 checks for $1, making the cost 10¢ a check. But a rival bank started selling 15 checks for $1. Now, logic tells me that because 15 is midway between 20 and 10, the checks should cost 7½¢ a check—midway between 5¢ and 10¢. However, when I divided 15 into $1, I find I am only paying 6⅔¢ cents a check! Why is this so? Why is the logical answer wrong?

G. W. Bartlett
Wheeling, West Virginia

Dear Reader:

That wasn't logic; that was intuition. And it's wrong in this case because Mother Nature didn't prepare us for long division. Here's the number 100 divided by 1 through 5:

$$100 \div 1 = 100$$
$$100 \div 2 = 50$$
$$100 \div 3 = 33\tfrac{1}{3}$$
$$100 \div 4 = 25$$
$$100 \div 5 = 20$$

Look at the divisors: $100 \div 1 = 100$, and $100 \div 5 = 20$, but you know perfectly well that 100 divided by 3 (the divisor midway between 1 and 5) isn't going to equal 60 (the quotient midway between 100 and 20)! As the divisor grows larger, its incremental effect on the quotient grows smaller, and here's a way to visualize it. Let's say you're going to build yourself a new house. If you get just one more person to help, the work will be divided in half, and the benefit will be huge. But if you already have a hundred people on the job, adding another will be of very small benefit.

• • •

Do any of you have a skeptical nature? Get your pen and paper ready. This next reply may prompt you to write to me.

Dear Marilyn:
Suppose you make $10,000 a year. Your boss offers you a choice. Either you can have a $1,000 raise at the end of each year, or you can have a $300 raise at the end of each six months. Which do you choose?
Ronald Gustaitis
Monroe, Connecticut

Dear Ronald:
Surprising, isn't it? The $300 raise continues to get better each year. At the end of one year, you'd be $300 ahead; at the end of three years, you'd be $700 ahead; and at the end of five years, you'd be $1,100 ahead. The cumulative total would be even higher ($3,500), and that's not counting interest.
The $300 semiannual raise increases not just your original earnings, but also each newly increased salary level so often that it easily overcomes the $1,000 yearly raise, which has slower growth. (Think of it as working for six months at a time instead of a year at a time.)

This is such a delightfully confusing concept that I knew even a full explanation would not suffice. (And yes, I find confusing concepts delightful.) Some people simply assume the answer is in error and wait for a correction, and other people write. And oh, did they ever write. But by the phrase "a $300 raise at the end of each six months," he doesn't mean that your annual wage goes to $10,300. He means that in the next six months you'll make $300 more than you did in the last six months.

Dear Marilyn:
Are you sure about your answer? I would love to use this example in class if I were convinced no error exists.
Arnold Barkman, Ph.D.
Texas Christian University
Fort Worth, Texas

There must be something I am overlooking, or there must be a typographical error in the column. I would appreciate a clarification if at all possible.
Cliff Hoofman
Senator, 25th District
North Little Rock, Arkansas

One thing is clear; it pays to know exactly what the boss means in offering you a choice.

Stephen Brown
Federal Reserve Bank
Dallas, Texas

Dear Readers:

The answer is correct, and the key is that it compares two different salary periods: a one-year period with a six-month one.

Let's say it's January 1, 1994, and you choose the $1,000 raise at the end of the year. For 1994, you earn $10,000. But if you choose the $300 raise, you earn $5,000 during the first six months and $5,300 during the second six months. For 1994, you earn $10,300.

With the $1,000 raise in effect for 1995, you earn $11,000. But with the $300 raise, you earn $5,600 during the first six months and $5,900 during the second six months. For 1995, you earn $11,500.

With the $1,000 raise in effect for 1996, you earn $12,000. But with the $300 raise, you earn $6,200 during the first six months and $6,500 during the second six months. For 1996, you earn $12,700.

With the $1,000 raise in effect for 1997, you earn $13,000. But with the $300 raise, you earn $6,800 during the first six months and $7,100 during the second six months. For 1997, you earn $13,900.

With the $1,000 raise in effect for 1998, you earn $14,000. But with the $300 raise, you earn $7,400 during the first six months and $7,700 during the second six months. For 1998, you earn $15,100.

It's surprising, and a good exercise for those of us concerned about economic factors like interest rates and how they compound.

● ● ●

Dear Marilyn:

Where can I find a table that would show us how long it takes our money to double at various interest rates?

William Muncie
Chambersburg, Pennsylvania

Dear William:

You don't really need a table. For a good approximation, just divide the number seventy-two by the interest rate, and the answer is the number of years it will take your money to double. For example, at 4.5 (percent), it takes about sixteen years. $(72 \div 4.5 = 16)$

● ● ●

Dear Marilyn:

My city has 50¢ tollbooths and 10¢ tollbooths. You can purchase a book of fifty toll tickets for $4 (8¢ apiece). When I use my tickets on the 10¢

booths, my friends say I'm losing money and that I should save the tickets for the 50¢ booths and go ahead and pay the 10¢ at the others. I say I'm still saving 2¢. Who's right?

Danny Denton
Richmond, Virginia

Dear Danny:
You're right. With no other factors to consider, you'll do better by using a ticket at every booth, no matter what the toll. Tell your friends that your way makes all tolls 8¢, but their way makes some tolls 8¢ and others 10¢. Here are some examples:

You all go through 100 booths; 50 at 50¢, 50 at 10¢. This costs you $8 (two books of tickets), but it costs your friends $9 (one book of tickets and 50 10¢ tolls). Or you go through 200 tolls: 50 at 50¢, 150 at 10¢. This costs you $16 (four books of tickets), but it costs your friends $19 (one book of tickets and 150 10¢ tolls). Or you go through 200 tolls: 150 at 50¢, 50 at 10¢. This costs you $16 (four books of tickets), but it costs your friends $17 (three books of tickets and 50 10¢ tolls). Your friends might be interested to note that the greater the proportion of 10¢ booths, the more *they* lose, not you!

•   •   •

Dear Marilyn:
My wife has a small sewing business and, with three sons, decided to trade services with a close female barber friend. She would sew for her and get haircuts free. Sewing is $8 an hour, and haircuts are $10 apiece, or for three boys—$30 an hour. My wife eventually found herself hours (even days) behind. To me, they should have matched hour for hour, not penny for penny. What do you think?

Dwayne Tannahill
Cottage Grove, Minnesota

Dear Dwayne:
I think there's a better compromise. As it is, the women assume that cutting hair is nearly four times as valuable as sewing. Is it? Or does the barber usually average only one or two haircuts an hour?

To get this "match" figure, look at the two women's yearly incomes and divide each one by the number of hours the woman works. If, for example, the barber made $24,960 last year, and she worked forty hours a week, she made $12 an hour (not $30). If your wife was always occupied with sewing work, as seamstresses so often seem to be, she made $8 an hour (or maybe more, if there were higher charges for specialized jobs).

At those rates, her friend could give all three boys a haircut in return for your wife's sewing for an hour and a half.

• • •

Dear Marilyn:

A woman's clothing store is having a sale on suits: If you purchase two suits at the full price, you receive a third suit at no charge. My daughter plans to buy two suits at $240 each. As for the free third suit, a friend wants to enter into this arrangement with her. She has found a suit she wishes to buy that is priced at the pre-sale price of $150. What amount should each girl pay?

Barbara C.
Monterey, California

Dear Barbara:

Before the sale, the three suits would have cost a total of $630. Of that, your daughter would have paid $480, or a little more than 76 percent, and her friend would have paid $150, or a little less than 24 percent. But now they'll only have to pay a total of $480 for all three suits (assuming that the $150 suit must be used as the "free" suit because it's of lesser value). Of that sale figure, your daughter's percentage would amount to $365.71, and her friend's would amount to $114.29.

• • •

Dear Marilyn:

Mike has two sons: Sam and Dave. He has one apple for them. Sam says he wants the whole apple. Dave says he would be content with half an apple. Mike splits the difference, giving Sam three-quarters of the apple and Dave one-quarter of it. Did Dave make a mistake?

Arthur Penser
Huntsville, Alabama

Dear Arthur:

If Dave actually wanted the whole apple, he made the mistake of misleading Mike. But if he truly wanted only half an apple, Mike alone made the mistake (which he did either way). He could have given Sam two-thirds of the apple and Dave one-third of it. Then each son would have gotten two-thirds of his wish.

• • •

Dear Marilyn:

If the price is the same, which is the better buy—a ten-inch round pizza or a nine-inch square pizza?

Roberto Morales
Bronx, New York

Dear Roberto:

It depends on whether you like the crust. If you're going to inhale the whole pizza, Roberto, the nine-inch-sided square one is a better buy than the ten-inch-diameter round one. But if you're going to throw away an inch of crust all around, you're better off with the round pizza. Oddly enough, even though a ten-inch circle has *less* area than a nine-inch square, an eight-inch circle has *more* area than a seven-inch square!

● ● ●

Dear Marilyn:

Let's say I have a bottle partly filled with soda, and I want to find out if it's half full. Which of the following would be needed? (1) Another bottle, (2) more soda, (3) a measuring cup, and/or (4) a scale?

J. L. Shelton
St. Petersburg, Florida

Dear Reader:

I wouldn't bother with *any* of them, if I were you. Just note the level of the liquid and turn the bottle over. (You can use your thumb to cap it, if necessary.) If it's half full, the soda will come up to that same level from the *other* end.

● ● ●

Dear Marilyn:

Which weighs more: a pound of feathers or a pound of gold?

Vinnie Haspersen
Bronx, New York

Dear Vinnie:

Try to remain calm, Vinnie. A pound of feathers weighs more! (I know you were trying to trick me into saying that a pound of gold weighs more, at which point you would say that a pound is a pound is a pound. But it isn't.) Not all pounds are created equal. Feathers are weighed in avoirdupois pounds, and gold is weighed in troy pounds. An avoirdupois pound is heavier.

Then we received the following letter from a reader.

Dear Marilyn:

I wonder how old Vinnie is. I dreamed up that question when I was in the eighth grade back in the late twenties in Fairfax, California, and I sent it in to Robert Ripley. He ran it in his feature, which in those days was on the comic pages, and it showed a pile of feathers next to a block of gold.

I used to spring that question occasionally. Most of the people would unthinkingly say "gold"; a few, more thoughtful ones, would say they're the same. Only the rare ones who knew about troy and avoirdupois weights would get it right.

That's how I was inspired to dream it up, studying the table of weights and measures on the back of my new school notebook.

Ted Chernin
Honolulu, Hawaii

• • •

Dear Marilyn:

Which weighs more: an ounce of feathers or an ounce of gold?

George Hollenbac
Houston, Texas

Dear George:

An ounce of gold weighs more than an ounce of feathers. That may see odd to readers who remember that I once said that a pound of feathers weigh more than a pound of gold, but it's true! "Not all pounds are created equal" was what I said, but "not all ounces are created equal," either. And befor a third person asks, a grain of feathers weighs the *same* as a grain of gol

The "grain" is the same in avoirdupois (used for weighing feathers) an troy (used for weighing gold.) But an ounce avoirdupois is 437.5 grains, an an ounce troy is 480 grains. And a pound avoirdupois is 7,000 grains, and pound troy is 5,760 grains. (And for any of you driving yourselves crazy o your home calculator with this, you should know that there are 16 ounce in a pound avoirdupois, but only 12 in a pound troy.)

I promise I won't mention this subject again. Really.

• • •

Dear Marilyn:

A briefcase has a three-wheel combination lock, and each wheel is num bered from zero to nine. How many possible combinations are there? An what are the odds against finding the correct combination?

Bill Shannon
Memphis, Tennesse

Dear Bill:

There are a thousand combinations involved, so you could say the chanc are only one in a thousand that you'd find the right one on the first try, b it actually would be fairly easy to try them all. If a briefcase has *two* of those locks, though, which many do (each with its own combination), the number jumps up to a million, and finding the correct set seems ten times more laborious—but again, it really isn't. You just open the first lock by rolling through the thousand combinations, then leave it open while you roll through the thousand combinations on the second lock.

● ● ●

Dear Marilyn:

Using letters and numbers, and a maximum of seven letters and numbers in combination, how many different license plates would that amount to?

John Giles, Jr.
Atwater, California

Dear John:

Assuming that we can use twenty-six letters and ten digits, there are 78,364,164,096 seven-character combinations—if you don't mind plates like ZZZZZZZ and 0000000. That's enough for more than 314 automobiles each for every man, woman, and child in the United States.

● ● ●

The following three "number facts," which close out this chapter, highlight their numbers in a new and different perspective. They're the three most surprising facts that have ever appeared in the column to date.

Dear Marilyn:

If the world population were gathered together in one spot, how large an area do you estimate we could cover?

Terry Wemple
Worcester, Massachusetts

Dear Terry:

With a world population of about 5.5 billion, if we allowed everyone a generous two-by-two-foot patch of ground on which to stand, they'd cover an area of less than eight-hundred square miles—only about the size of Jacksonville, Florida. Surprisingly small, isn't it?

● ● ●

Dear Marilyn:

How much of the land in the United States is used up for roads?

Jim Brock
Galesburg, Illinois

Dear Jim:

Brace yourself, Jim. This isn't going to be a pleasant thing to hear. According to the Federal Highway Administration, there are 3,871,000 miles of roadway in the country. If we take 50 feet as an average road width, including shoulders, this translates to an utterly staggering 36,657 square miles of land used for this purpose—more than the entire state of Indiana!

● ● ●

Dear Marilyn:

What was the magnitude of manpower involved in the Persian Gulf War? Didn't we overdo it? Iraq isn't a big country.

Joel Fitz
Danbury, Connecticut

Dear Joel:

Prepare yourself for a surprise. There were more people attending Paul Simon's 1991 concert in Central Park (upwards of 750,000) than the entire number of coalition forces in the Persian Gulf—including Americans, Saudis, British, Egyptian, and French (altogether about 744,000).

Seventeen

M A T H   P U Z Z L E S

Dear Marilyn:

Years ago, I was offered an airplane if I answered ten teasers in ten seconds each. I flunked. Here's one of them: If a dog weighs ten pounds plus half its own weight, how much does it weigh? And why? (Remember, you have only ten seconds.)

Frank McCafferty
Tempe, Arizona

Dear Frank:

It weighs twenty pounds; ten pounds plus ten pounds—half its own weight of twenty pounds—equals twenty pounds. (Say, you wouldn't happen to remember the name of that fellow who offered you the airplane, would you?)

This kind of problem often bothers people even after they've read the answer, so we published another version at a later date.

Dear Marilyn:

I've had a lot of fun with the following question, and hardly anyone has been able to figure out the answer: If a brick weighs three pounds plus half a brick, how much does a brick and a half weigh?

Marjorie Lakin
Ocala, Florida

Dear Marjorie:

Nine pounds. If a brick weighs three pounds plus half a brick, then a brick weighs six pounds (three pounds plus half of six pounds). So a brick and a half must weigh nine pounds (six pounds plus half of six pounds).

• • •

Dear Marilyn:
Let's say that I've just been to the audio store and spent half my money in half an hour. I now have as many pennies as I had dollars before, but only half as many dollars as I had pennies before. How much did I spend?
Mel Brosnan
Oceanside, California

Dear Mel:
It's a good thing you didn't stay twice as long. As it is, you spent $49.99. You started with $99.98 and have $49.99 left, with 99 pennies now compared to 99 dollars before and with 49 dollars now compared to 98 pennies before.

• • •

Dear Marilyn:
I solved this problem by the trial-and-error method but have had no success solving it mathematically. Can you help? This is the problem: I want to take 100 people to the circus, and I have $95.00 to spend. Admission for men is $10.00, for women $2.50, and for children, $.50. How many of each can I take?
Fred Bullock
Cerro Gordo, North Carolina

Dear Fred:
Then you know that the answer is 2 men, 13 women, and 85 children. Here's a hint to solve it mathematically: There can't be 5 men because they'd cost $50 to take, and even if all the remaining $45 were spent on children, you'd only be able to bring a total of 95 people (5 men and 90 children) instead of 100.
The number of people would continue to decrease if you were to take even more men, so that narrows the possibilities to just 1, 2, 3, or 4. Start from there, and discard any answers that call for people to be divided into pieces. (You're not the magician!)

• • •

Dear Marilyn:
A census worker asks a lady for the ages of her three children. She replies that the product of their ages is 36, and the sum of their ages is the same as the address next door. After looking at the next-door address, the census

worker returns and says that he needs more information. The lady agrees to give one final clue and says, "The oldest is sleeping upstairs." What are the ages of the children, and what is the address next door?

Hugh Fisher
Baton Rouge, Louisiana

Dear Hugh:

Assuming that there are no children of the same age in years who aren't twins (and that no twin is considered "older") the children are 2, 2, and 9, and the address is 13. The following are the only combinations of three ages whose product is 36.

$$1 \times 1 \times 36 \qquad 1 \times 6 \times 6$$
$$1 \times 2 \times 18 \qquad 2 \times 2 \times 9$$
$$1 \times 3 \times 12 \qquad 2 \times 3 \times 6$$
$$1 \times 4 \times 9 \qquad 3 \times 3 \times 4$$

Except for two of the combinations, their sums are all different, so the census worker would have been able to determine the ages of the children if the address next door had been any of those six different ones. As he needed more information, however, the address must have been 13, shared by two combinations: 1, 6, 6, and 2, 2, 9. So when the mother indicated that there was an oldest child, she eliminated the first combination, which had *two* "oldest," leaving 2, 2, and 9 as the only possible answer.

● ● ●

Dear Marilyn:

Seven cats can kill seven rats in seven minutes. How many cats will it take to kill a hundred rats in fifty minutes?

Vernon Hutton
South Bend, Indiana

Dear Vernon:

"Fourteen cats" is probably the answer you want. If the seven cats act together, killing a rat a minute, that same group would kill fifty rats in fifty minutes—so a group twice that large would kill a hundred rats in fifty minutes.

But the question isn't really well-defined because it doesn't specify that the cats are acting together. What if it takes each of seven cats a full seven minutes to kill a rat apiece? Then each cat would kill only seven rats in fifty minutes. (You can't kill one-seventh of a rat, so the cat would have a minute to spare.) In that case, fourteen cats would kill only ninety-eight rats in fifty minutes.

All fourteen of the cats would have a minute to spare and would be watching two rats still running around. If the cats changed tactics at that point and acted as a group, we might not have a problem. But the question doesn't state how the cats behave, so the answer "fourteen cats" isn't as satisfying as it could be.

●   ●   ●

Dear Marilyn:

I've never seen this puzzle anywhere, so I hope you'll enjoy it: A friend of mine takes me for a drive through a small town with one thoroughfare and ten across streets. On the way, he hands me a pad and pencil and asks that I quickly note the street signs as we pass. I note 8, 5, 4, 9, 1, 7, 6, 10, 3, and 2. Then my friend says, "Don't put your paper down yet. Now we're entering the neighboring town. Note the street signs just like you did before." This time I note 8, 5, 1, 4, 9, 2, 7, 6, 10, and 3. Looking at the pad, I say, "What's going on in those towns, anyway?" My friend smiles and says that the arrangement of signs is perfectly reasonable. Can you deduce why the signs are arranged the way they are?

> Eric Kongs
> Wilmington, California

Dear Eric:

Those weren't the nice little towns of Cardinal and Ordinal, were they? The cardinal numbers (indicating quantity) in alphabetical order are eight, five, four, nine, one, seven, six, ten, three, and two. The ordinal numbers (indicating order) in alphabetical order are eighth, fifth, first, fourth, ninth, second, seventh, sixth, tenth, and third.

●   ●   ●

Dear Marilyn:

When you travel to work going 60 mph, you arrive there early. When you travel to work going 30 mph, you arrive there late. The amount of time you are early is also the amount of time you're late. How fast should you go to get to work on time?

> Stan Zelinger
> Mission Viejo, California

Dear Stan:
   Assuming you're stubborn about leaving at the same time each day, and discounting such things as acceleration and deceleration time, you'll have to shoot out the driveway at 40 mph and come to a screeching halt in the parking lot at work to be right on time.

● ● ●

Dear Marilyn:
   Suppose you have an airplane that is able to fly 100 mph (relative to the air), and you need to make a round-trip flight from city A to city B two hundred miles away. You want to make this trip in the shortest possible time. Today the winds would be a 50 mph tailwind from A to B, and the same 50 mph headwind from B back to A. Tomorrow the winds will be calm. Should you make the trip today or tomorrow, or would both take the same time?
                                                   Mandley Johnson, Jr.
                                                   Bismarck, North Dakota

Dear Mandley:
   You should go tomorrow, when there's no wind, and it'll take you four hours. Going with the matching tailwind and headwind will cost you an extra hour and twenty minutes.

After this reply appeared, we received the following letter from a reader, a pilot since 1959, who interpreted the question somewhat differently:

Dear Marilyn:
   I agree with the elapsed-time portion of your answer. However, I would suggest you take off as soon as you possibly can *today*, which would save you an entire day, over waiting until tomorrow to take advantage of the flight conditions. The only advantage in waiting would be to conserve fuel.
                                                   George Lewis
                                                   Sonoma, California

But this next pilot, no doubt quite a bit younger, insisted (erroneously) that I was wrong. (And to think, we make the older pilots retire!)

Dear Marilyn:
   My girlfriend asked me to answer your question because I'm an airline pilot. Predicated on 100 mph *airspeed*, it makes no difference.

Your answer was correct had the problem stipulated 100 mph *ground-speed* because wind affects groundspeed; it doesn't affect airspeed.

Name Withheld

City, State Withheld

I've withheld this fellow's name to spare him the embarrassment not just of getting the problem wrong (although it shouldn't be a difficult problem for a pilot) but also for confusing airspeed and groundspeed (which I'm sure he has discovered by now)!

• • •

Dear Marilyn:

Maybe the wind blew the stamp off the envelope while it was en route to you. I wrote months ago and have been waiting anxiously for your reply. Take any number—301, for example.

$$
\begin{array}{rr}
\text{Add 7.} & +\ \ 7 \\ \hline
 & 308 \\
\text{Multiply by 2.} & \times\ \ 2 \\ \hline
 & 616 \\
\text{Subtract 4.} & -\ \ 4 \\ \hline
 & 612 \\
\text{Divide by 2.} & \div\ \ 2 \\ \hline
 & 306 \\
\text{Subtract your original number.} & -301 \\ \hline
\text{The answer is always the same:} & 5!
\end{array}
$$

Regardless of what number you choose, it always works. Why?

Richard Kennedy

Carson City, Nevada

Dear Richard:

When you add 7 to the number, then multiply it by 2, this has the effect of adding 14 to your multiplied number. Then you subtract 4 from the total, leaving only 10 added to your multiplied number. So when you divide it all by 2, you return to your original number plus that extra 10 divided by 2. And 10 divided by 2 is 5, so when you subtract your original number at the end, you're always left with 5.

• • •

The following kinds of problems are difficult for nearly everyone. Most people don't know how to begin to solve them, and because the problems look so darned intimidating, they don't even try. But that's mainly because most people have never been exposed to this kind of thinking, so it looks foreign to them. This is why I've solved the next two problems step by step and written them all out so you can follow it along. If you're game to give it a try, you'll gain increased mental mastery by the time you're finished. (And if you're not game, well, just skip right on to the next chapter. I'll never know!)

Dear Marilyn:
 Using any of the numbers ∅ through 9, substitute a number for each letter in the following addition problem:

```
    H O C U S
+   P O C U S
    ─────────
  P R E S T O
```

Grant Pinney
Lake Isabella, California

Dear Grant:
 First, P is 1, because the two numbers added can't be more than 199998. This means that R is ∅ because even if H were 9, and 1 were carried, R must be 1 or less.

```
    H O C U S
+   1 O C U S
    ─────────
  1 ∅ E S T O
```

S must be 2, 3, 4, 6, 7, 8, or 9; it can't be 5 because O can't be ∅. This limits O to 2, 4, 6, or 8. H must be 8 (if 1 was carried) or 9. But if H were 8, O would be 6 (to produce 1 to carry), which means that S would be 3, and that means that C would be 6 as well, so that's impossible. So H is 9.

```
    9 O C U S
+   1 O C U S
    ─────────
  1 ∅ E S T O
```

O must be 2 or 4 (because 6 or 8 would produce 1 to carry); this limits E to 4, 5 (if 1 was carried), or 8, and it limits S to 2, 6, or 7. But S can't be 2 because then O would be 4, which means that C would be 1 (to avoid carrying); as that's impossible, S is limited to 6 or 7. But S can't be 7 because then O would be 4, and E would 8, leaving only 2, 3, 5, and 6 for C, U, and T; U could be only 2 or 6; if it were 2, making T a 5, this leaves only 3 or 6 for C, which is impossible if S is 7 (because nothing was carried); likewise, if U were 6, making T a 3, this leaves only 2 or 5 for C, which is impossible if S is 7. So S is 6, making O a 2.

```
    9 2 C U 6
+   1 2 C U 6
    ─────────
  1 ∅ E 6 T 2
```

T is odd (because 1 was carried), so it must be 3, 5, or 7. But it can't be 3 because then U would be 1 or 6; and T also can't be 5 because then U would be 7 (and nothing can be carried). So T is 7, making U a 3 (because nothing can be carried). The last unused digits are 4, 5, and 8. C must be 8, and E must be 5. Here's the final answer:

```
    9 2 8 3 6
+   1 2 8 3 6
  1 Ø 5 6 7 2
```

•   •   •

Dear Marilyn:

Here's my favorite math problem. (The reason for showing the zero at the end is to indicate that the division comes out even.) Can you solve it?

```
          XX8XX
    XXX)XXXXXXXX
         XXX
         XXXX
          XXX
          XXXX
          XXXX
             Ø
```

Tom Kilby
Mission Viejo, California

Dear Tom:

The last digit of the quotient must be 9 because 8 times the divisor equals only a three-digit number in line No. 3, but line No. 5 has four digits. Also, there must be two Ø's in the quotient on each side of the 8 because two numbers (instead of just one) had to be "brought down" to lines No. 2 and No. 4. The divisor must be 124 or less because 8 times the divisor equals only a three-digit number. Given that, the first digit of the quotient must be more than 7 because 7 times the highest-possible divisor of 124 equals a three-digit 868 for line No. 1. But the lowest possible first four digits of the dividend are 1000, leaving a three-digit initial remainder for line No. 2 instead of its two-digit one. However, it must be less than 9 because 9 times the divisor in line No. 5 is four digits, not three. This means that 8 is the first digit of the quotient. With a quotient of 80809, the divisor must be more than 123 because the dividend is eight digits long. Therefore, the divisor must be 124.

With that the case, here's the rest of the problem:

```
                       80809
                124)10020316
No. 1                 992
No. 2                1003
No. 3                 992
No. 4                1116
No. 5                1116
                        0
```

Are you still there? Hello? Hello?

Eighteen

Dear Marilyn:

Five angry cowgirls, standing in a field, accuse each other of rustling. No two distances between any pair of women is the same. Each has one bullet in her gun. At the count of ten, each shoots her nearest neighbor in the toe. Will each cowgirl be shot, or will at least one escape injury?

Martin Gardner
Hendersonville, North Carolina

Dear Martin:

How nice to hear from the master of mathematical puzzles himself! Let's say Tammy and Loretta are the closest distance apart; each will shoot the other in the toe. This leaves Dolly, Naomi, and Wynonna. If one (or more) of them shoots Tammy or Loretta, then only two (or fewer) bullets are left for Dolly, Naomi, and Wynonna, so at least one must escape injury.

Or maybe none of them shoots Tammy or Loretta. In that case, we can forget about those two, and consider just the other three. Of Dolly, Naomi, and Wynonna, let's say Naomi and Wynonna are the closest distance apart; each will shoot the other in the toe. This leaves Dolly. She'll shoot either Naomi or Wynonna, but there'll be no bullet left to shoot Dolly, so again, one cowgirl will escape injury.

• • •

Dear Marilyn:

An island is populated by natives, most of whom have brown eyes; the others have blue eyes. As the natives meet every day, each knows the eye color of the others, but because talking about eyes is taboo, none knows the color of his or her own eyes. One day, a medicine man comes to shore to heal the sick. After seeing everyone, he says that he cannot cure anyone because not everyone has brown eyes. The natives then vow that when anyone finds out that s/he has blue eyes, that person will leave the island at the end of the day. Hearing this, the medicine man proclaims that he will return on the first day the island is all brown-eyed again. On a future morning, the natives see his boat returning. They look around and discover that he is fulfilling his promise; it is their first day without any blue-eyed people. How did the medicine man know when to return?

Eugene Hamori
New Orleans, Louisiana

Dear Eugene:
The medicine man can return after the number of days passes that equals the number of people he saw with blue eyes. That is, if the day of his visit was day No. 1, and he saw nine people with blue eyes, he can return on day No. 10. For example, if only one person has blue eyes, s/he'll see no others and therefore will leave at the end of day No. 1, so the medicine man can return on day No. 2. And if two people have blue eyes, each will see only one other; if that other isn't gone at the end of day No. 1, they know they must both leave at the end of day No. 2, so the medicine man can return on day No. 3. Likewise, if three people have blue eyes, each will see only two others; if both aren't gone at the end of day No. 2, they know they must all leave at the end of day No. 3, so the medicine man can return on day No. 4, and so forth. That is, all of the blue-eyed people will leave on the same day; once they've gone, all the rest will know they have brown eyes.

What a politically incorrect medicine man. In 1994, he'd get sued for every last bottle of firewater left in his boat.

I hope I don't hear from "Cannibals Anonymous" on this next one, accusing me of insensitivity toward people whose appetites just happen to be a little different from everyone else's.

Dear Marilyn:
There are three missionaries and three cannibals who must cross a dangerous river. The rowboat can hold only a limit of two people. All the missionaries can row. Only one cannibal can. At no time can you have more cannibals than missionaries on one side of the river, for obvious reasons. Can you get them all across safely?

Bob Russell
Sarasota, Florida

Dear Bob:
I see only one way to do it at the moment, and even then, we have to count on having helpful, cooperative cannibals.

Two cannibals head for the far shore; one rows back. Then two head for the far shore again, and one rows back. Then two missionaries head for the far shore. At this point, we have one missionary and one cannibal (who can row) on the near shore, and two of each on the far shore.

One of each row back. When they arrive, the cannibal who can't row gets out, and the cannibal who can row gets in. Then the missionary and the cannibal (who can row) head for the far shore. And at this point, we have one missionary and one cannibal on the near shore, and two missionaries and two cannibals (one of whom can row) on the far shore.

The cannibals want to take a break for lunch, but the missionaries promise them poor boys for dinner if they wait, so one of each row back. The cannibal gets out, the remaining missionary gets in, and two missionaries head for the far shore. And at this point, we have two cannibals on the near shore and three missionaries on the far shore, along with the cannibal who can row.

The cannibal who can row is beginning to get cranky, so the missionaries promise him ladyfingers for dessert, and the rest is easy. He rows back and picks up one cannibal from the near shore, takes him to the far shore and leaves him, then rows back and picks up the last cannibal for the final trip.

But maybe there's another way. (If you try this yourself, however, remember that cannibals can never outnumber missionaries, not even when getting in and out of the boat.)

Well, I haven't heard from any cannibals yet, but I did receive the following letter from a fellow who seems to be a sort of food critic:

Dear Marilyn:

I do not like your answer to the cannibal/missionary problem. Your premise that two cannibals can be left alone assumes that cannibals will only eat noncannibals. This supposes that either (1) the cannibals are lifelong friends from the same tribe (who would never do that to one another), or (2) cannibals have a code of honor that forbids them from eating other cannibals. Extensive research on my part revealed the true cannibal creed: Meat is meat, and when I'm hungry, I eat.

Peter Erlichson
St. Louis, Missouri

Hmmm. I don't personally know any cannibals to ask, but if cannibals routinely ate each other, there wouldn't be too many cannibals left, would there? (Then again, maybe that's why I don't know any cannibals!)

● ● ●

Dear Marilyn:

In the following puzzle, every fact is relevant and must be considered in the solution: A train is operated by three men—Smith, Robinson, and Jones.

They are a fireman, an engineer, and a brakeman, not necessarily in that order. On the train are three businessmen of the same names—Mr. Smith, Mr. Robinson, and Mr. Jones.

1. Mr. Robinson lives in Detroit.
2. The brakeman lives halfway between Chicago and Detroit.
3. Mr. Jones earns $26,000 a year.
4. Smith beat the fireman at billiards.
5. The brakeman's neighbor, one of the passengers, earns three times as much as the brakeman, who earns $10,000 yearly.
6. The passenger whose name is the same as the brakeman's lives in Chicago.

Who is the engineer? We don't know the correct solution and have been working on this for several years now.

Jo and Jerry Kolpek
Mason City, Iowa

Dear Jo and Jerry:

The engineer is Smith, and here's why:

As Smith beat the fireman at billiards, Smith must be either the engineer or the brakeman.

The brakeman's neighbor, one of the passengers, earns three times as much as the brakeman, who earns $10,000 yearly. So the brakeman's neighbor must not be Mr. Jones, who earns $26,000 a year.

Mr. Robinson lives in Detroit. Because the brakeman lives halfway between Detroit and Chicago, and his neighbor is not Mr. Jones, the neighbor must be Mr. Smith. And as one of the passengers lives in Chicago, that passenger must be Mr. Jones.

As the passenger whose name is the same as the brakeman's is the one who lives in Chicago, the brakeman's name must be Jones. And, as we said at first, Smith must be either the engineer or the brakeman, so if the brakeman's name is Jones, the engineer's name must be Smith.

• • •

Dear Marilyn:

A professor tells his assistant that he dined with three people the previous night. He also tells her that the sum of their ages is twice that of the assistant's and that the product of their ages is 2450. He asks her to tell him the ages of the three people. After a while, the assistant tells the professor that she doesn't have enough information to solve the problem. He agrees and says that he is older than any of his dinner companions. The assistant then promptly gives the professor the ages of the three people. What are their ages? (All must be in whole years.)

Maurice Janco
Santa Barbara, California

Dear Maurice:

Maybe they all went out for hamburgers. The ages seem to be 49, 10, and 5. (The professor is 50, and the assistant is 32.)

There are twelve age groups whose product is 2450:

1, 25, 98	2, 25, 49	5, 7, 70	7, 7, 50
1, 35, 70	2, 35, 35	5, 10, 49	7, 10, 35
1, 49, 50	5, 5, 98	5, 14, 35	7, 14, 25

All have different sums (which means that if any of those sums had been twice the assistant's age, she would have known the diners' ages) except two groups: 5, 10, 49 and 7, 7, 50.

Then the professor added that he was older than any of his dinner companions. Because that information was helpful, the professor must not have been 51 or older. And he couldn't have been 49 or younger, or he wouldn't have been old enough. This leaves the age of 50, making the professor older than anyone in the 5, 10, and 49 group (but not in the 7, 7, and 50 group).

● ● ●

Dear Marilyn:

There are five books on a shelf. Each book has 100 pages. A bookworm starts eating on the first page of the first book. From there he eats in a straight line through to the last page of the last book. Through how many pages did the bookworm eat?

David Denton
Plainview, Texas

Dear David:

He ate a hole through 302 pages.

I gave that short answer half to tease people and half to make them visualize the problem themselves. But when they did, they disagreed with me! The following column was the result.

Dear Marilyn:

Okay! What's with this darn bookworm? My husband refuses to discuss it any more, my friends are losing sleep, and my sons are ready to have me committed! Please explain how you came up with the answer of 302 pages.

Sari Balfour
Palm City, Florida

Help! It's driving me batty.

Russell Taylor
Spring, Texas

Was the answer a misprint?

Carol Bealefield
Houston, Texas

Wouldn't the answer be 152 pages? There are two numbers on each page. A 100-page book only contains 50 pages, so if the bookworm ate through 302 pages, it would really just be 152.

Nick Riley
Stoneham, Massachusetts

Your answer of 302 pages assumes he is an English-speaking bookworm who eats from left to right. If he were a Jewish bookworm, he'd eat from right to left and would, therefore, consume 500 pages.

Debbie Jordan
Cumming, Georgia

How do you know the worm's gender? Why is it a "he" rather than a "she"? In defense of the opposite sex, please explain.

G. Ray Arnett
Stockton, California

Dear Readers:

English books are shelved from left to right, so the first page of the first book is on the right of it (as you look at the binding), and the last page of the last book is on the left. For that reason, the bookworm need only eat one page of the first volume, all pages of volumes two, three, and four, and only one more page of the last volume—a total of 302. Here's an illustration:

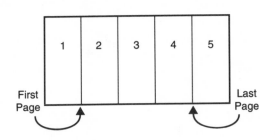

No matter how you define a page, the answer is still 302, because you can't switch definitions in midstream. If a book has 100 of "them," whatever they are, and we ask through how many of "them" did the bookworm eat, the answer must use multiples of 100, not 50.

And an Eastern bookworm would eat the same number of pages if the books read from right to left, were paginated from "back" to "front," and shelved from right to left. Here's the path she would take:

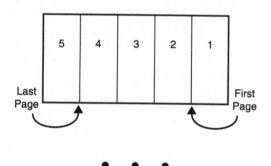

• • •

Dear Marilyn:

My wife insists that our bathroom scale is on the high side. She says she weighs only 132 pounds! The only sure method I could find for testing the scale was our dog, a beagle, recently weighed by our vet at 33 pounds. We put him on the scale four times and got the total of 135 pounds instead of 132 pounds. My wife exclaimed, "See! What'd I tell you!" Looking for hidden variables, I asked, "When did you feed him last?" She said, "About an hour ago." Well, that was the answer! I told her to let him outside for a while and then we'd weigh him again. I intended to weigh him only once and multiply the result by four. But this last time as I struggled to get him into the bathroom, he snarled at me and ran under the bed. Do you have any suggestions?

Thomas Burrichter
New Port Richey, Florida

Dear Thomas:

Yes. Take your wife to the vet and have her weighed.

Nineteen

VISUAL PUZZLES

Dear Marilyn

A friend of mine gave me a version of the drawings below. By cutting the square along the lines indicated and rearranging the pieces into the rectangle shown, one gets an extra bit of area. If these were three-dimensional figures with a height of one inch, there is, of course, an added cubic inch of volume. My friend hopes to perform this trick someday with a block of gold and increase his wealth. All the math says that it works, but there is no way that he will end up with more gold—or is there?

L. Paul Dickerson
Warrenton, North Carolina

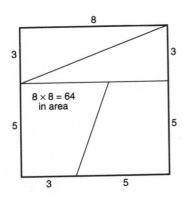

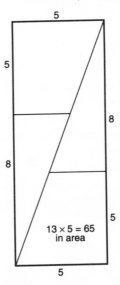

Dear Paul:

I hope you guys haven't been planning on this for your retirement. The pieces in the figure on the left look close enough to the pieces in the figure on the right to fool the eye. They're even close enough to fool the hand. If you try to duplicate them on a one-inch scale, cutting them out and piecing them together, they appear to fit. But they don't. You must do it *extremely* carefully to find a long, narrow gap between them, a gap that would fill— you guessed it—about one square inch.

●　●　●

Dear Marilyn:

Here's a puzzle for you: In the rearranged triangle, can you explain where the extra square comes from?

Oly Oltjenbruns
St. Louis, Missouri

(A)

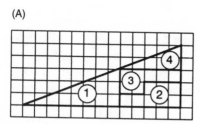

(B)

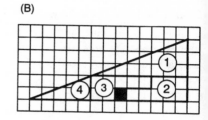

Dear Oly:

It comes from slivers of three of the transplanted pieces (No. 1, No. 3, and No. 4) from (A) that were shaved off to fit them into their new positions in (B). (Piece No. 2 remained the same size.) It's deceptive because the eye doesn't readily discern the difference.

●　●　●

Dear Marilyn:

Let's say circle A is stationary and has a circumference of three inches. Circle B is free to roll around the perimeter of circle A and has a circumference of one inch.

If circle B, starting at point C, rolls completely around the perimeter of circle A, returning to point C, how many revolutions will it have made?

Woody Wooldridge
Tampa, Florida

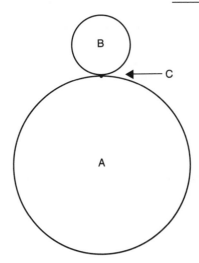

Dear Woody:

If we see B as a small coin with a figure on it, its feet at C, it will turn four somersaults on its axis as it traces a path around A before returning to its starting position.

I knew my readers would love this one, but I was unprepared for the cascade of cardboard circles, gears, drawings, photographs, circular sections of wood, and the like. It looked like a crafts fair in my office for weeks. I was also surprised that the following response column then generated as much mail as the original did.

Dear Marilyn:

We, Mr. Frear's geometry class, are writing to you about the circle problem. We found your answer, "It will turn four somersaults on its axis as it traces a path around A before returning to its starting position," extremely surprising. Could you explain or correct it?

Damascus High School
Damascus, Maryland

What? What? What? I cut out little circles of paper and rolled them around each other. I've looked at this problem logically, illogically, and every other way. It's three times, period.

Christine Lamut
Evanston, Illinois

This drove me nuts. I used a quarter and a wine glass base, and the coin made it around three times. But I could be wrong. Maybe I should have just filled the wine glass and forgotten about it. After all, I'm the nut who ran around with dental floss measuring the circumference of everything in my kitchen.

Cathi Betancourt
Selden, New York

Help! Since your circle column, I haven't slept a wink! Please publish more soon so I can get some sleep!

Joseph Gray
Spring Lake, North Carolina

After an unbelievable amount of study, deductive reasoning, meditation, and prayer, I'm at a complete loss to understand your answer, and so are two friends who were honor graduates of Georgia Tech and Auburn University.

James Altman
Gray, Georgia

I have a feeling that the post office might get rich this week. But please don't let this one little mistake worry you.

Jack Roberts
Salt Lake City, Utah

I hope the Japanese press will not find out about this.

Josef Biela
Anaheim, California

You're wrong, but you're still my favorite "Marilyn."

Ken Sangrey
West Palm Beach, Florida

Dear Readers:

Wow. Out of all that mail, I found only *one* letter that agreed with me, and here it is: "I always enjoy reading your column, and this one created a bit of work for me. I received several requests for confirmation or confutation. As (nearly) always, you were correct." (James Williams, Jr., Ph.D., SEPTE Professor of Engineering, Head, Mechanics and Materials Division, Department of Mechanical Engineering, M.I.T.)

Here's an illustration to show how it works. (Get out the dental floss and wine glasses, everybody!)

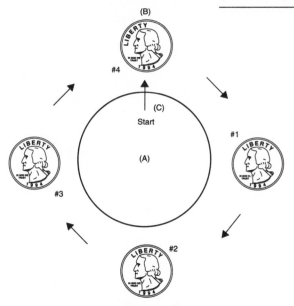

Shortly afterward, I received the following letter from a reader.

Dear Marilyn:

Did you know that the Scholastic Aptitude Test (SAT) writers got your little-circle-rolling-around-the-big-circle problem incorrect in the 1982 version of the SAT?

According to the book *Calculus with Analytic Geometry*, alternate edition by Earl Swokowski of Marquette University (for which I had the job of writing the solutions manual), the SAT folks did not include four (the correct answer) among its choices. ("To the embarrassment of the Educational Testing Service of Princeton, New Jersey, this [4] was not one of the choices given as an answer.")

I hope this adds a little interest to the large file you are no doubt collecting on this problem.

> Stephen Rodi, Ph.D.
> Division Chairperson
> Mathematics and Physical Sciences
> Austin Community College
> Austin, Texas

According to published reports, scores on the mathematics section of the SAT, taken by three-hundred thousand high-school students, had to be recalculated.
A year and a half after we ran the original problem, we published the following question and answer with some trepidation.

Dear Marilyn:

Try this one: Say circle A is stationary and has a circumference of three inches. Circle B is free to roll around the inside of the perimeter of circle A and has a circumference of one inch. If circle B, its starting point at C, rolls completely around the inside of the perimeter of circle A, returning to point C, how many revolutions will it have made?

> Anne Blackwell
> Cahaba Heights, Alabama

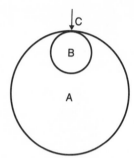

Dear Anne:

Are you trying to drive my readers crazy? Yes, the answer is two, and here are their positions:

The trepidation was well-founded. In order to avoid publishing a reply column, I'd included a diagram the first time, but it apparently wasn't convincing enough. More letters (and cardboard circles, gears, drawings, photographs, circular sections of wood, and the like) soon arrived. Here are excerpts from a few of them:

Dear Marilyn:

Sometimes I'm not sure about your logic in solving a puzzle, and I just shrug it off and figure you know what you're doing. Sometimes I look at the clock and figure that it's just too early on a Sunday morning to worry about it, anyway. However, it's after noon now, and I'm wide awake, and I have no excuses.

If the circles were made of string, and you unraveled the smaller circle as it rotated so that it stuck to the larger circle, wouldn't you run out of string at the four o'clock position?

I may not sleep at all this week, and I'm starting a new job tomorrow!

Larry Gomberg
Burtonsville, Maryland

Surely you goofed! If not, you can't leave such a cliffhanger—all of us would give up on you or go crazy. Please, please explain. I can't stand it.

Gene Jackson
Walnut Springs, Texas

I can only assume that someone on the staff handled this question while half asleep.

Nancy Hall
Annapolis, Maryland

Then, just as I was wondering what to do about it all, the following letter arrived.

Dear Marilyn:

I enjoy reading your column each week, and I was particularly intrigued by the circle-rolling-inside-another-circle problem that was published. One way to explain your result is to borrow a line from the Irish Blessing: "May the road rise up to meet you . . ." In effect, the "road" on which the smaller circle travels is the larger circle, which "rises up" (that is, it curves upward), producing a smaller angle through which the smaller circle must rotate during each small incremental step, as it rolls around the interior of the larger circle, than if the rolling took place on a flat surface. (On a flat surface, the circle would roll one revolution for each perimeter distance, but this is true only if the surface is flat.) Add up these incremental steps, and you get exactly the result you published.

Professor Puttaiah, Chair of our Mechanical Engineering Department, points out that the circle-rolling-outside-another-circle problem is related to ones that occur in engineering when we are designing gear configurations. The "inside" problem you proposed applies to planetary gear trains.

I offer to help your readers visualize the geometry of the problem by sending copies of this letter (with additional detailed explanations and accompanying diagrams) to anyone who sends a self-addressed, stamped envelope. Keep up the good work.

William Gregory, Dean
Leonard C. Nelson College of Engineering
West Virginia Institute of Technology
Montgomery, West Virginia

Thanks for the help, Dr. Gregory!

• • •

This next puzzle had been sent by dozens of readers before, but I'd always passed it by because it's impossible to solve. Finally, it occurred to me that people might like to know that!

Dear Marilyn:
This puzzle has my family stumped: The trick is to have a continuous line going through each and every side only once. And you can't have the line touching or crossing over itself.

Kathleen Durkin
Natick, Massachusetts

#1	#2	#3
#4	#5	

Dear Kathleen:
Don't feel bad. Judging from the number of times I've received this puzzle, it has *plenty* of people stumped. But it's impossible to solve it, and this is why: Take a look at rectangles No. 2, No. 4, and No. 5. Each is bounded by an odd number of line segments. That means each has to have a line either begin inside it or end inside it. But there are *three* of them, and a continuous line only has two ends!

• • •

Dear Marilyn:
A fly is on the centerline of the twelve- by twelve-foot end wall of a 30-foot-long room. He is one inch up from the floor. A spider is on the centerline

of the opposite wall one inch down from the ceiling. What is the shortest path from the spider to the fly? (The spider never leaves a room surface, and the fly doesn't move.)

W. B.
Boynton Beach, Florida

Dear Reader:
It's forty feet, and here's the path from the spider to the fly.

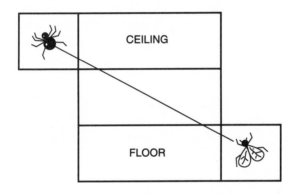

Now, you can't possibly write me about that *one, can* you?!

Twenty

Dear Marilyn:

Someone told me that a self-made person would be happy with his material wealth because he earned it, but a person who won millions of dollars in the lottery would not be happy because it was unearned. Do you think this is true?

> Bill Walker
> Boston, Massachusetts

Dear Bill:

Oh, I wouldn't go so far as to say *that!* But let me go on record here as saying that I am ethically opposed to lotteries and other large-scale forms of gambling for many reasons—mainly because money is given by those who can't afford it to those who don't deserve it, with only false hope in return. Even so, I think most of us feel good about receiving money; the difference is that those of us who actually earn it also feel good about *ourselves*.

● ● ●

Dear Marilyn:

Do you feel that a lottery's history can predict its future winning numbers?

> S. Davis
> Greensboro, North Carolina

Dear Reader:

It's not a matter of feeling; it's a matter of fact. Unlike people, a lottery's past is totally irrelevant to its future.

• • •

Dear Marilyn:
For years, I have been playing the same lottery numbers and never won a cent. Would I have more chance to win if I play different numbers instead of always playing the same ones

Edward Wilson
Brooklyn, New York

Dear Edward:
Assuming there's no connection between one lottery and the next one, no. Your chances are exactly the same. But it doesn't *help* to play the same numbers, either.

• • •

Dear Marilyn:
I play the same five numbers without fail in the lottery. I know that the mathematical odds of winning start over with each drawing, but do you agree that sooner or later, nearly every combination of numbers will have come up? (Hope so!)

Peggy Hafner
St. Paul, Minnesota

Dear Peggy:
I see what you're getting at. Yes, given an unlimited amount of time, every number eventually will be chosen. But the flaw in this reasoning is that every number eventually will be chosen equally often. Theoretically, this means that if there are a million different number combinations, you'll have to buy a million tickets while waiting for your number to turn up once. And because lottery payoffs are less than their receipts, you'll lose money this way. That's why lotteries are held. Overall, the purchasers of tickets lose more money (which goes to whoever runs the lottery) than the individual winners gain.

Another way to look at this is that the lottery doesn't remember which numbers have already won once (or twice or three times) and thus know to avoid them, so no particular number has a better chance the next time. In fact, other numbers are more likely to win two or even many times before every single number wins even once.

• • •

Dear Marilyn:

In a lottery, are the odds any greater against the same six numbers coming up in a particular drawing that had come up in the drawing immediately preceding it?

Henry Temple
North Haven, Connecticut

Dear Henry:

No. If everything else is equal, the odds are the same. Remember, unlike you, the lottery has no memory.

• • •

Dear Marilyn:

My son-in-law and I have a disagreement on the lottery. He thinks the odds of winning the lottery are just as good when you pick the numbers in sequence (1-2-3-4-5-6) as they are scattered (3-6-15-20-39-43). But I've played the lottery for many years, and I've never heard or seen six numbers drawn in sequence. Please settle our dispute.

Richard Ciesielski
Fort Wayne, Indiana

Dear Richard:

The odds are the same. The reason people remember fewer winning "sequence" numbers is that, depending on the lottery rules, there are usually fewer of them than there are "scatter" numbers. However, when you buy a lottery ticket with a scatter number, you don't get *all* the scatter numbers; you only get *one*. This means that while the odds that *some* scatter number will be chosen are greater than *some* sequence number, the purchaser of a *particular* scatter ticket doesn't get those same odds.

Here's a way to illustrate it. Let's say there are six numbers in the lottery and two numbers on a ticket, all sold. The tickets would look like this ("sequence" numbers enclosed):

(1-2)	(2-1)	3 1	4 1	5 1	6 1
1 3	(2-3)	(3-2)	4 2	5 2	6 2
1 4	2 4	(3-4)	(4-3)	5 3	6 3
1 5	2 5	3 5	(4-5)	(5-4)	6 4
1 6	2 6	3 6	4 6	(5-6)	(6-5)

There are twice as many scatter numbers (twenty) as there are sequence numbers (ten), but picture them all (thirty) written on slips of paper and dropped into a box. The chances of picking out any *one* ticket are still one in thirty.

• • •

Dear Marilyn:
    You said once that a ticket purchaser who based his selection on the birthdates of family members didn't decrease his chances of winning and that the numbers he eliminated were no different from the numbers anyone else eliminated. However, he eliminated these numbers on a systematic basis, and no one else did. This must make some difference. If not, could you please show me the error in my thinking?
                                                    Michele Leimgruber
                                                    Demarest, New Jersey

Dear Michele:
    It can make a difference, but not in his chances of winning, and the kind of difference depends on how the lottery is constructed. If the prize is a million dollars, and a million different tickets are sold, with the winner to be drawn from among those, it doesn't matter which ticket he purchases.
    But let's say those million people get to *choose* their ticket numbers, the prize to be split among any duplicates. A total of 999,999 people pick No. 7, and you pick No. 11. The winner is drawn from the numbers 1 through 1,000,000. While the chances are equal that No. 7 and No. 11 will win, you'd have a much better payoff with No. 11 than all those people sharing No. 7. In this kind of setup, avoiding "popular" numbers is a wiser bet.

• • •

Dear Marilyn:
    Our lottery decreased the chances for the big prize from 14-million-to-1 to 24-million-to-1. Can you put those odds in perspective? For example, what are the chances of being hit by lightning?
                                                    Edward Knaudt
                                                    San Diego, California

Dear Edward:
    I wouldn't get your hopes up. At those odds, the chances of being struck by lightning sometime this year are about forty times *greater* than the chances of winning any one lottery.

• • •

Dear Marilyn:
    During a recent get-together, a group of us were discussing the lottery. Let's say the chances of winning the top prize are 1 in 7 million. I and another engineer said that if you buy two tickets, your chances of winning are 2 in 7 million (or 1 in 3.5 million). The only other engineer in our group said that mathematically our logic is not correct. He said that with the first ticket the chances are 1 in 7 million, and the second ticket only changes

the chances to 1 in 6,999,999, and the third ticket to 1 in 6,999,998, and so on. Do we buy him a drink, or do we make fun of his ethnic heritage?

W. J. Banulski
Southington, Connecticut

Dear Reader:

Well, maybe can just get him to buy *you* a drink, instead; it's less risky to your health than making fun of his ethnic heritage! You're right, and here's a way to illustrate what's wrong with your friend's argument: He says that the second ticket changes the chances to 1 in 6,999,999, and the third ticket to 1 in 6,999,998, etc., but continue to buy more tickets mentally to see what eventually happens to the mathematics.

Removing one more from the total each time means that the 6,999,999th ticket you buy would make your chances of winning just 1 in 2! Now, that can't be right, can it? You buy 6,999,999 tickets, and your chances of winning are only 1 in 2?!

● ● ●

Dear Marilyn:

If I only have ten dollars to spend on the next ten drawings of the lottery, and the chances of winning are 1 in 13 million (each time), wouldn't it be most advantageous to bet all the money at once? It seems that raising the odds for one drawing would give me a much better chance of winning than betting one dollar on ten different lotteries. Am I correct? Incorrect? This has been driving me nuts!

Angeline O'Brien
Racine, Wisconsin

Dear Angeline:

It's the same either way. Although it may seem at first that buying the ten tickets all at once gives you a better chance because the betting pool will be smaller (13 million in just that one lottery instead of ten times that number in all of them), don't forget that over the course of the ten lotteries, there also will be ten prizes, not just one.

● ● ●

Dear Marilyn:

Would you settle an argument? My father plays the "numbers" (our state's is the lottery). He says there are "good numbers" and "bad numbers." I disagree. My logic is that they cannot be rated when they change daily and nobody knows what they are until they are drawn. What do you think?

Reneè Poeschl
Pittsburgh, Pennsylvania

Dear Reneè:
   You're right. And you're also right to equate playing the lottery with playing the "numbers." Although the government benefits from lotteries, the money that goes to the owner of a racetrack, for example, has never been the reason that playing the "ponies" has long been associated with personal ruin. It's the money lost by the gamblers, and lotteries absorb far more of that now than racetracks (and other gambling venues) ever have, effectively bringing gambling to the masses and reaching far more of them than ever before.

• • •

Dear Marilyn:
   Suppose you enter a contest where 150 tickets are sold and placed in a container. The tickets are drawn one at a time, and the last ticket drawn is the winner. What are the chances of winning?
                                          J. Wilson
                                          Wilmington, North Carolina

Dear Reader:
   One out of 150—the same as if the *first* ticket drawn were the winner. There's just a little more suspense this way.

• • •

Dear Marilyn:
   I play gin rummy with a group of men who claim cards get "ginned out" after two or three games, no matter how many times they're shuffled. ("Ginned out" means the cards are dealt in the sequence of past hands, and players are dealt two or three spreads or nearly gin hands.) Is this possible?
                                          Harry Ilaria
                                          Bloomfield, New Jersey

Dear Harry:
   Sounds like "ginned *in*" to me (as in "broken in"), not "ginned *out.*" But either way, it's not true. Current thinking has it that seven ordinary shuffles mix a deck thoroughly. (Fewer aren't enough, but more don't help that much.) So maybe you guys just aren't shuffling enough!

• • •

Dear Marilyn:
   Please respond as soon as possible because I'm down to my last dollar. Why can't I win money at the racetrack? I've been a bettor for fifty years, and I've acquired handicapping skill and have spoken with horse owners,

trainers, jockeys, stable hands, bookmakers, and hundreds of other bettors, who are also losers. Why?

Name Withheld
San Diego, California

Dear Reader:

You're all in the same boat, really. Unlike gambling in a casino, when you place a bet at the track, you don't bet against the house. The house, in fact, doesn't give a darn whether you win or lose. That's not how they make their money. Instead, you bet against the other bettors. And that's why it's so difficult to win money overall, no matter how knowledgeable you become.

Here's how it works: The people bet their money, the track takes a flat percentage (in New York, it's 17 percent), and the remainder is distributed among the winners. So every dollar that passes into the betting windows comes back out as only eighty-three cents (or so). That's a tough percentage to beat, even if you're very sophisticated. And all your sophisticated friends reduce your winnings even more. Your best bet would be to go to a track when everyone (but you) was a novice. And there aren't any tracks like that.

There are quite a few readers who sign themselves "Anonymous" even when asking the most innocuous questions; maybe they're just shy. That last reader wasn't. She signed her full name and address, but I withheld it in order to spare her any possible embarrassment. Imagine my surprise when she wrote to complain! Here's her second letter, which I promised her I would publish in this book, complete with her name.

Dear Marilyn:

I was enlightened when I read your answer to my question. More so, I was very excited that you considered it good enough to print. But I was disappointed that you removed my name. I'll bet the chances of my letter getting published were one in a million. I hope the chances of a reprint are not one in a billion.

Annette Glassman
San Diego, California

● ● ●

Dear Marilyn:

Here's a roulette question that drives me and my friends nuts. If we're playing roulette on a wheel that has thirty-eight slots, the probability of the ball dropping into any one specified slot is one out of thirty-eight, right?

But let's say we use two balls at once. Assuming that they'll fit easily, what's the probability of both balls dropping into any one slot together?

Mike Guider
Richmond, Virginia

Dear Mike:

It's still one out of thirty-eight. The first ball "specifies" the slot, and the second ball has a one out of thirty-eight chance of dropping into it.

• • •

Dear Marilyn:

Let's say we're playing roulette, and I offer you a bet: You can pick any triplet of black and red—say red/red/black or red/black/red. Then I'll pick a different one. At the starting point, we'll watch each spin of the roulette wheel until one of our triplets appears as a run. If yours comes first, you win. If mine comes first, I win. Even chances, right? But I'll give you three-to-two odds! When you win, I pay you three dollars, but when I win, you only pay me two dollars. We'll play as many times as you like, and you can always have the first choice. Will you take the bet?

George Groth
Hendersonville, North Carolina

Dear George:

What a great "sucker" bet that would be! No, your chances of winning would range from two-thirds to seven-eighths, depending on what triplet I choose. You would always be able to choose a triplet with a better chance of winning. Let's use the seven-eighth chances as an example because it's the most obvious. There are eight different triplet cominations, and let's say I choose black/black/black. If it appears at the start, I win, and that'll happen one-eighth of the time. But before it appears any time afterward, it would have to be preceded by a red. So if you choose red/black/black every time I choose black/black/black, you'll win seven-eighths of the time!

• • •

Dear Marilyn:

What are my best odds? Winning the lottery, you answering this letter, or getting a raise?

Leetha Lundstrom-Wehner
Kailua-Kona, Hawaii

Dear Leetha:

If I were you, I think I'd ask for a raise next time.

Twenty-one

PROBABILITY
AND CHOICE

Dear Marilyn:

There is a single path up a mountain. A climber starts about 6 A.M. and arrives at the top around 6 P.M. He stays there overnight, starting down the next day about 6 A.M. and arriving at the bottom around 6 P.M. On each day, he travels at varying speeds—enjoying the scenery, stopping for lunch, and so on. What are the chances that there was a spot on the mountain path that he passed at exactly the same time both days?

Jerry Biel
Englewood, Florida

Dear Jerry:

It's 100 percent, and here's how to visualize the proof: Imagine both the climber's trips taking place at once. The climber starts up at the same time his "twin" starts down. At some point along the way, regardless of whether one stops for lunch and the other doesn't stop at all, they will undoubtedly meet as they pass each other. That will be the place and time.

● ● ●

Dear Marilyn:

A meter reader has 315 meters to read. One meter reads 476300. The next meter in succession reads exactly the same. What is the probability of this occurring?

Wendell Reed
Sedona, Arizona

Dear Wendell:

From my point of view, it's relatively high, and here's why: Every day brings mail from people who relate similar "against-the-odds" occurrences— ranging from running into an old friend on the other side of the world to discovering a serial number matching a social-security number. If you had specified the event *before* it occurred, the odds against it would be enormous. But as you only specified it afterward, it becomes simply another ordinary coincidence. That is, you only noticed whatever *did* occur, no matter what it was, and the odds of *something* occurring at some point in your life are quite high by comparison.

•   •   •

Dear Marilyn:

After each holiday-gift exchange, my five nieces and nephews write their names on slips of paper and put them into a basket from which they then draw the name of the person for whom they'll buy a gift the following year. This year, for the first time, *each of the five drew his or her own name*, much to the amazement of us all. What are the chances of such an occurrence taking place?

Richard Coffey
Newington, Connecticut

Dear Richard:

It's unlikely, of course, but the chances aren't as low as you might think— about 1 in 120.

•   •   •

Dear Marilyn:

While attending a lecture on fire safety in the home, the speaker said, "One in ten Americans will experience some type of destructive fire this year. Now, I know that some of you can say that you have lived in your home for twenty-five years and never had any type of fire. To that I would respond that you have been lucky." He then went on to say, "But that only means that you are not moving farther away from a fire, but closer to one." Is his last statement correct? Are those people moving closer to a fire?

David Smith
Lufkin, Texas

Dear David:

No. Moreover, people who have never had a fire are even somewhat *less* likely to have one than average, but for such nonstatistical reasons as the use of successful precautions or engaging in less high-risk behavior. For example, people who don't smoke seldom experience a mattress fire.

•   •   •

Dear Marilyn:

On some standardized tests where there is a penalty for guessing, the following rule applies:

Question answered correctly: 1 point awarded
Question left blank: 0 points
Question answered incorrectly: ¼ point deducted

Is the following argument sound? On a question with five possible choices, there is a one-fifth chance of guessing correctly. Therefore, the effective penalty for guessing is one-fifth less one-fourth, which equals minus one-twentieth.

Patricia Keifer Foster
Charlotte, North Carolina

Dear Patricia:

I don't see this as a "guessing penalty" because if the correct answers are randomly spread over all five choices, then for every five shot-in-the-dark guesses, you'll gain one point (accidentally getting one correct) and lose one point (one-fourth each for four wrong ones), which will not affect your accumulated total awarded for real knowledge. It also means that if you make only wild guesses throughout the entire test, even though one-fifth of those will happen to be correct, your score will be zero, as it should be. It's not perfect, but it's a good system. To sum it up, if you have any idea what an answer should be, be sure to guess. But if you have no idea, it doesn't matter what you do.

• • •

Dear Marilyn:

My psychology class received the following question:

Threatened by a superior enemy force, the general faces a dilemma. His intelligence officers say his soldiers will be caught in an ambush in which all six hundred of them will die unless he leads them to safety by one of two available routes. If he takes the first, four hundred soldiers will die. If he takes the second, there's a one-third chance that none will die, and a two-thirds chance that six hundred will die. Which route should he take?

The answer we were given was that it doesn't matter because the chances are the same in either case. The wording is supposed to trick you into thinking there's a difference. But many of us in the class failed to follow this line of reasoning. Is there a mathematical solution to this?

J. Cooke
Honolulu, Hawaii

Dear Reader:

If we were talking about civilians, and if the intention of the general were simply to save as many lives as possible, and if this choice were to be repeated again and again, then no, there would be no difference mathematically. But you received this question in psychology class, not math class, and armies are not created to save their own lives. They have other objectives, often requiring significant sacrifice of life. For example, if only the survival of two hundred soldiers is required to secure a particular location and win the war, the general should take the first route. But if three hundred are required, he must risk the second.

• • •

Dear Marilyn:
  I select an envelope from two envelopes, knowing that one envelope (but not which one) contains twice as much money as the other one. I find a hundred dollars in my first selected envelope. Should I switch to the other one to improve my worldly gains?

Barney Bissinger
Hershey, Pennsylvania

Dear Barney:
  This is a dandy paradox. While it appears as though you should switch because you have an even chance for $200 versus $50—which any gambler would grab—it actually makes no difference at all. Those even chances would apply only if you could choose one of *two* more envelopes, one with $200 and the other with $50. As it is, there's just one more envelope sitting there, with either twice the amount you've already seen or half of it. And you knew that would be the case before you even started. So when you opened the first envelope, you didn't gain any information to improve your chances.
  This can be illustrated by noting that the logic that causes you to switch (because you appear to have an even chance for $200 versus $50) will lead you to switch *every* time (no matter what you find in the first envelope), making the second envelope just as randomly chosen as the first one!

One reader replied with the following, effectively highlighting the emotional/intellectual aspect of the choice.

Dear Marilyn:
  I am asked to select one of two very large containers and told only that one contains a billion trillion times as much gold dust as the other. I find a hundred dollars worth of gold dust in the container I select. Should I switch to the other one to improve my worldly gains?

Richard Burton
Hot Springs, South Dakota

The chances in this situation are the same as in the original; you'll just be more excited about playing the game. Let's say that you can pay a dollar to have a one-in-ten chance at two dollars. You won't want to bet. But what if you can pay a dollar to have a one-in-ten chance at a million dollars? You'll bet, of course. But whether the game is a good bargain doesn't affect the chances of your winning. They're still one in ten either way.

● ● ●

Dear Marilyn:

Three of us couples are going on a vacation this coming weekend. We're staying away two nights, and we've rented two studios because each holds a maximum of only four people. One couple will get its own studio on Friday, a different couple on Saturday, and one couple will be out of luck. We'll draw straws to see which are the two lucky couples.

I told my wife that we should just draw once, and the loser would be the couple out of luck both nights. I figure we'll have a two out of three (66⅔ percent) chance of winning one of the nights to ourselves. But my wife contends that we should draw straws *twice*—all three couples on Friday and the remaining two couples again on Saturday. She reasons that a one-in-three (33⅓ percent) chance for Friday and a one-in-two chance (50 percent) for Saturday will give us better odds.

I told her to look at it like a drawing for $10 million and asked if she would rather have a 66⅔ percent chance of winning a single drawing, or a 33⅓ percent chance in one drawing and a 50 percent chance in a second. Which way should we go?

Dave Phillips
Heber City, Utah

Dear Dave:

Actually, it's the same either way. Your chances couldn't increase relative to any other couple because you'll all be in the same drawing.

I didn't do a second column on this issue, but there were still plenty of people wondering about it, so I'll explain:

First, envision three straws in a hat, one green one marked "Friday," one green one marked "Saturday" and a red one marked "unlucky." Everyone draws at once, and the issue is settled. That's the kind of drawing the husband chose.

Now envision the same three straws in a hat. Everyone draws at once, but the couple with "Friday" holds onto their straw for a day. Then the other two are put back into the hat, and the remaining couples choose between them. That's the kind of drawing the wife chose.

But it's no different than if the second and third couples had just held onto their "Saturday" and "unlucky" straws in the first place, as above. (Except that they might switch positions with each other.)

When you draw once for a "loser," you may be trying for two nights, but you'll always split the pot. That means you have a one-third chance for "Friday" and a one-third chance for "Saturday."

When you draw twice for "winners," it's the same. You have a one-third chance for "Friday" and "Saturday" alike, not one-half for "Saturday." This is because you won't be participating in the "Saturday" drawing at all if you win on "Friday," which will be one-third of the time. So you'd only have two-thirds of those one-half Saturday chances, and two-thirds of one-half equals one-third—the same as with the other method of drawing.

●　　●　　●

The following scenario is fairly will known, but because it so often clashes with intuition, I decided to focus on the intuitive aspects of it.

Dear Marilyn:

I've heard that it doesn't take very many people at all in a group—maybe a dozen or so—before there are two people with the same birthday, month, and day. Why wouldn't people's birthdays follow the rules of random probability?

Kathy Menell
Columbus, Indiana

Dear Kathy:

Oh, but they do. (For the purposes of this problem, we assume that people's birthdays are spread evenly throughout the year instead of being clumped for any reason.) And according to those laws, if 23 people get together in a random grouping, the probability is a shade greater than fifty-fifty that at least two of them will share the same birthday. (Still, that just means that half the time they will, and half the time they won't. Not such a big deal, really.)

Many people think that it would take 183 people to tip the odds past fifty-fifty, and the difficulty in "seeing" why this is wrong may come from our forgetting just how unlikely it would be for everyone to have a *different* birthday. Remember—any of the people can match with any other. Envision 100 people at a meeting; you ask all of them not only to silently choose a number between 1 and 365, but also to try to select one that no one *else* is choosing. Wouldn't it be utterly astonishing if every single one of those people did indeed pick a different number? Well, that was only 100 people, not 183, and they were *trying*!

●   ●   ●

Dear Marilyn:

We have three young children—all boys. Lots of people tell us to "try one more time, the odds are you'll get a girl this time!" Are the odds fifty-fifty with each pregnancy, or do you consider the sex of the children you already have?

K. S.
Minneapolis, Minnesota

Dear Reader:

The odds start all over again each time, just as they do with each flip of a coin. Relatively few people have three boys (out of three), all right, and even fewer people have four boys (out of four), but at this stage in your life as a parent, you've got a fifty-fifty chance of becoming one of the latter!

●   ●   ●

Dear Marilyn:

Here's a problem that may pose a challenge: Do men have more sisters than women have? (And do women have more brothers than men have?) That is, each person doesn't count himself (or herself), so, for example, in a family of two children—a boy and a girl—the boy has a sister but no brother, and the girl has a brother but no sister. Likewise, in a family of four children—two boys and two girls—each boy has two sisters but only one brother, and each girl has two brothers but only one sister.

Ruma Falk, Ph.D.
The Hebrew University of Jerusalem
Jerusalem, Israel

Dear Ruma:

Strange as it may seem, men and women have an equal number of sisters and brothers. This is because repeatedly choosing at random one child from a family and noting how many sisters and/or brothers he or she has amounts to randomly removing one child from all families and simply counting the females and males left. Assuming an even male/female distribution of the sexes, these numbers will be about the same.

A great many readers wrote to insist that my answer was incorrect, but for a further explanation, I'll defer to Dr. Falk, an expert on the subject, who later sent the following additional explanation:

Let's agree to assume equal probabilities for male and female births and independence among births (whether in different families or within the same family). These are no hypothetical assumptions; they reflect biological reality fairly accurately.

Most people expect men to have more sisters than women have and more sisters than brothers. They reason that because, on the average, families have an equal number of sons and daughters, the set of siblings of men, who are themselves *not counted*, should comprise an excess of women (sisters). This apparently compelling reasoning is nevertheless wrong! Men are expected (in the long run) to have the same proportion of sisters as women have, and the same proportion of sisters as brothers.

Asking a child from a family of, say, seven children how many brothers and how many sisters he or she has, is equivalent to picking a random family of six children and asking how many sons and how many daughters it has. In the latter case it is obvious, however, that one should expect (over many such families) the same proportion of sons and daughters. Hence, irrespective of whether the questioned individuals are males or females, they would have, *on the average*, the same number of brothers and sisters. This is the *essence* of the idea of *independence*: the probabilities of male or female childbirth in the respondent's family are *not affected* by knowledge of the respondent's gender.

● ● ●

Dear Marilyn:

You have a hat in which there are three pancakes. One is golden on both sides, one is brown on both sides, and one is golden on one side and brown on the other. You withdraw one pancake, look at one side, and see that it is brown. What is the probability that the other side is brown?

Robert Batts
Acton, Massachusetts

Dear Robert:

It's two out of three. The pancake you withdrew had to be one of only two of them: the brown/golden one or the brown/brown one. And of the three brown sides you could be seeing, two of them also have brown on the other side.

I especially enjoyed all the mail that arrived afterward, which consisted of hundreds of letters from perfectly serious people making perfectly serious arguments about . . . pancakes!

Dear Marilyn:

I look forward every week to your column, but I disagree with your analysis of the "three pancakes in a hat" question. I believe the chances are fifty-

fifty. Since we know that we hold one of two, and the other sides are either brown or gold, it is equally likely that either color shows up when we flip our pancake over. Don't you agree?

Elmer Mooring, Jr.
Johns Hopkins University
Baltimore, Maryland

Your answer about the pancakes is wrong. It should have been one chance in two. Only two pancakes have brown sides, and one of them has brown on only one side. There is a 50 percent chance that you are looking at the one with brown on both sides. I have been told that you have never publicly admitted to being wrong. Is this true?

R. Larry Marchinton, Ph.D.
University of Georgia
Athens, Georgia

Dear Readers:

No, that's not true. So don't worry. Whenever I'm wrong, I announce it in this column loud and clear. Some readers are still certain that earlier probability answers are wrong and that I simply won't admit an error. But that's not the case. A probability error hasn't occurred (yet!), and this one wasn't an exception. The original answer is correct. Note that it's easier to discover a brown side on a brown/brown pancake than on a brown/gold pancake.

Here's another way to look at it. Before you pull out any pancake at all, what are the chances that you'll pull out a pancake with sides that match? They're two out of three, right? So if you pull out a pancake and see a gold side, the chances that the other side is also gold is two-thirds. Likewise, if you pull out a pancake and see a brown side, the chances that the other side is also brown is two-thirds.

● ● ●

Dear Marilyn:

Three prisoners on death row are told that one of them has been chosen at random for execution the following morning, but the other two are to be freed. One privately begs the warden to at least tell him the name of one other prisoner who will be freed, and the warden relents. "Susie will go free," he says. Suddenly horrified, the first prisoner says that because he is now one of only two remaining prisoners at risk, his chances of execution have risen from one-third to one-half! What should the warden do?

Marvin Kilgo III
Camden, South Carolina

Dear Marvin:

Going home and not coming back until the following afternoon sounds like a pretty good idea. Even though there are only two remaining prisoners at risk, the first prisoner still has only a one-third chance of execution. Oddly enough, however, things don't look so good for the other prisoner, whose chances have now gone up to two-thirds!

And yes, plenty of mail arrived on that one, too. Here is a sampling of the letters:

Dear Marilyn:

You have done it again! I must strongly recommend that you either get a new reference or take a course (beginning college level) in probability. The prisoner's chances for execution did indeed go from one-third to one-half. People believe what you say, so give them correct information.

Stephen Van Fossan, Ph.D.
San Diego, California

You cannot correctly apply feminine logic to odds. The new situation is one of two equal chances.

Charlie Paine
Richmond, Virginia

Well, there's no such thing as feminine logic, and the original answer is correct. The questioning prisoner had a one-third chance of execution, and we've learned nothing to change that; however, we have learned something about the two others. Because they'll include the doomed prisoner two-thirds of the time, and because the warden will never name that one, the prisoner who isn't named has that two-thirds chance of execution.

● ● ●

Dear Marilyn:

The Greens and Blacks are playing bridge. After a deal, Mr. Brown, an onlooker, asks Mrs. Black: "Do you have an ace in your hand?" She nods. There is a certain probability that her hand holds at least one other ace. After the next deal, he asks her: "Do you have the ace of spades?" She nods. Again, there is a certain probability that her hand holds at least one other ace. Which probability is greater? Or are they both the same?

Martin Gardner
Hendersonville, North Carolina

Dear Martin:

How delightful to hear from the master of mathematical puzzles again! Mrs. Black's second hand—the one with the ace of spades—is more likely to have another ace, and here is my own explanation: There are fewer opportunities to get a particular ace than there are to get any ace at all. But each of these groups of opportunities contains an equal number of "golden" opportunities to get more aces. Therefore, the smaller group provides the greater chance of success. (Maybe you could blue-pencil this reply and send it back to me.)

Well, it needed blue-penciling, all right. See the following letter, which I wrote to "Ask Marilyn."

Dear Marilyn:

I've noticed a weakness in one of your answers. Also, I know you've been waiting for a reader to identify it so that you can correct it in print, but as it looks like that may never happen, I thought I'd better write a letter myself!

In the question, two couples are playing bridge. After a deal, an onlooker asks a player if she has an ace, and she nods; after another deal, he asks if she has the ace of spades, and she nods. After which deal is it more likely that she has at least one other ace? Or are they the same?

Marilyn vos Savant
New York City

Dear Marilyn:

That wasn't a weakness, Marilyn, that was an error! (But thanks for being so polite.) I replied that the hand with the ace of spades is more likely, and that's correct. But the explanation was wrong; it was intended to illustrate the principle behind the answer by applying it to an idealized two-ace game, but I failed to mention that.

I said there are fewer opportunities to get a certain ace than to get any ace at all. But each of these groups contains an equal number of ways to get more aces, so the smaller group provides the greater success ratio. Try this with a four-card "deck," two aces and two other cards, dealing two cards each to two players, and you'll see the principle at work.

• • •

Dear Marilyn:

Let's say that an older segment of our society is plagued by four different ailments. The percentages of that population having each of these are 80 percent, 75 percent, 70 percent, and 70 percent. At least what percent of this population is plagued with all four ailments?

Barney Bissinger
Hershey, Pennsylvania

Dear Barney:

No one need have all four illnesses. But if that's the case, 95 percent of the people have three illnesses, and 5 percent have two.

It was time to get out the blue pencil again.

Dear Marilyn:

When you answered the question, "If a population is plagued by four ailments, and the percentages having each are 80 percent, 75 percent, 70 percent, and 70 percent, at least what percentage has all four?" you correctly stated that the least is 0 percent. However, you went on to say that in that case, 95 percent have three illnesses, and 5 percent have two. This is incorrect. If 0 percent have four illnesses, and if *exactly* 95 percent have three, *then* the remaining 5 percent have two.

W. Hugh Haynsworth
Charleston, South Carolina

Dear Hugh:

Right you are. I should have said, "No one need have all four. But if that's the case, at least 95 percent have three. And if that's also the case, 5 percent have two. (The sound you hear, Hugh, is that of millions of heads being scratched.)

Twenty-two

The ability to understand the laws of numbers—probability and statistics, in the case that follows—affects how we operate within an enormous array of everyday issues and concerns, both professional and personal. This next question is a real-world application of that understanding.

Dear Marilyn:

A particularly interesting and important question today is that of testing for drugs. Suppose it is assumed that about 5 percent of the general population uses drugs. You employ a test that is 95 percent accurate, which we'll say means that if the individual is a user, the test will be positive 95 percent of the time, and if the individual is a nonuser, the test will be negative 95 percent of the time. A person is selected at random and given the test. It's positive. What does such a result suggest? Would you conclude that the individual is highly likely to be a drug-user?

Charles Feinstein, Ph.D.
Santa Clara University
Santa Clara, California

Dear Charles:

Given your conditions, once the person has tested positive, you may as well flip a coin to determine whether s/he's a drug user. The chances are only fifty-fifty. (The assumptions, the makeup of the test group, and the true accuracy of the tests themselves are additional considerations.) This is just the sort of common misunderstanding that should give great pause to those who will make the decisions about testing.

• • •

Dear Marilyn:

I read your column on random drug tests, and it hit home very hard. I am a truck driver. I went for a random drug test and showed a false positive. This has cost me my job, and I am now in a drug-rehabilitation program. Neither my boss, the union, the clinic that gave the test, nor the Department of Transportation will even consider the possibility of a false positive. I desperately need to know more to try to save my job and clear my record.

> Name Withheld
> Chicago, Illinois

As Professors of Statistics, we found your response to the drug-testing question perplexing and, indeed, incorrect. Another way of framing the question is, "Out of all the people who test positive, what percentage are actual users?" On the first test, the correct response is 95 percent, meaning that the test is incorrect only 5 percent of the time. This is *not* a fifty-fifty proposition. We would also argue that the test should be given twice. The likelihood of error on two consecutive tests is only twenty-five times out of ten thousand. We hope you will readdress this.

> Paul Susen, Ph.D.
> Herman Gelbwasser, Ph.D.
> Mount Wachusett Community College
> Gardner, Massachusetts

What we should be concerned about is the probability of a nonuser being wrongly classified, and this probability remains at 5 percent. A second drug test would decrease this probability of misclassifying a nonuser to one-fourth of 1 percent. We'll take the risk.

> Eric Villavaso, Ph.D.
> Gerald McKibbin, Ph.D.
> U.S. Department of Agriculture
> Mississippi State, Mississippi

Next time you respond to such a question, I think you should keep your political views to yourself.

> Steve Kovler
> Monroe, New York

Dear Readers:

Urging understanding among those who will make the decisions about testing isn't a political statement. This is a complex and important issue; study is required. Drug-testing is a powerful tool, and like all powerful tools, it must be handled with care. Simply eating poppy-seed pastry can make a person test positive for morphine. So will a cough syrup containing codeine. Even over-the-counter drugs cause a similar problem.

The original "fifty-fifty" answer is correct. Also, it often doesn't help to repeat the same test because the false reports aren't random. Instead, they're more likely to come from analytic sensitivity (the proportion of positive results in actual positive samples) and analytic specificity (the proportion of negative results in actual negative samples), and these are determined by biochemical factors, not statistical ones. *That is, we're not referring to "lab error."*

Here's how the "fifty-fifty" answer is determined. Suppose the general population consists of 10,000 people. Of those people, we assume for this problem that 95 percent of them (9,500) are nonusers and that 5 percent of them (500) are users.

Of the 9,500 nonusers, 95 percent of them (9,025) will test negative. That means 5 percent of them (475) will test positive. Of the 500 users, 95 percent of them (475) will test positive. That means 5 percent of them (25) will test negative. These are the totals:

9,025	true	negatives	(non-users)
475	false	positives	(non-users)
475	true	positives	(users)
25	false	negatives	(users)
10,000	total	population	

There are 475 "false positives" and 475 "true positives"—a total of 950 positives—so when we find an individual in that positive group, there's only a fifty-fifty chance s/he's a user.

But let's suppose instead that a randomly chosen person tests negative. From the above, we can see that there are 25 "false negatives" and 9,025 "true negatives"—a total of 9,050 negatives—so for an individual in that *negative* group, there's an overwhelming chance (more than 99 percent) that is s/he is *not* a user.

Here's another letter:

Dear Marilyn:

Your answer regarding drug-testing is correct. Drug-testing should not be done in this fashion because the results of testing may affect employment, liability, etc. There are about 105 laboratories certified by the Forensic Urine Drug Testing Program and/or the National Institute of Drug Abuse. In these laboratories, the specimens that test positive in the screening procedure are retested for confirmation by an even more specific method, raising the predictive value of a positive test.

It is vitally important that your readers understand that the situation described by your reader may exist if testing is done outside of a certified laboratory, such as an employer or a noncertified laboratory. This situation does not occur if testing is done by a certified laboratory.

David Mulkey, M.D.
W. Howard Hoffman, M.D.
David Miller, M.D.
Peter Scully, M.D.
Desert West Drug Testing Consultants
Las Vegas, Nevada

Dear Readers:

Suppose the overall performance goes all the way up to 99 percent instead. Is *that* good enough? No! The Centers for Disease Control (CDC) state that the two tests (enzyme immunoassays or "EIA" and Western blots or "WB") combined have better than a 99 percent overall analytic performance accuracy rate in identifying human immunodeficiency virus type 1 (HIV-1), but only if they're taken repeatedly. (The actual rate is unknown.) This rate is the percentage of correct test results in all specimens tested. With a 99 percent rate, if a population of 10,000 were tested, 9,900 would receive correct results, but 100 would receive erroneous results—either false positives or false negatives, including indeterminates.

The CDC also state that of the errors, they have no data on how many are false positives versus false negatives. However, if we use 99 percent as an example, the false positives would have to be less than four-tenths of the erroneous results because the CDC estimates that .4 percent of Americans are "HIV positive." That is, if false positives accounted for fully four-tenths of the errors, then the .4 percent of people who are HIV positive would all be false positives, and we know that's not the case.

Let's try assuming that false positives are only two-tenths of those errors, leaving false negatives accounting for the remaining eight-tenths. So, of those same 100 people with erroneous results, 20 percent would have false positives and 80 percent would have false negatives. While those "false-negative" people would be an unwitting threat to sex partners, at least most people are aware that "negative" doesn't mean "safe."

But there's another ramification: The CDC estimate that .4 percent of Americans are "HIV positive." In a population of 10,000, that's 40 people. But that number must include all the false positives, which we assumed to be 20, leaving only 20 people actually infected. This leads to an interesting conclusion.

In this 99 percent scenario, there are as many "false positives" as there are "true positives." Even if both the AIDS tests results (EIA and WB) are positive, the chances are only fifty-fifty that the individual who took them is actually infected. That's why people with HIV-positive results must be sure to get tested repeatedly over the following months. The error rate is high with only two tests. (The CDC's Morbidity and Mortality Weekly Report shows an overall performance rate of only 97.1 percent on the Western Blot alone, far worse than our example.) Even after years, you may not fall ill. You may not have AIDS at all. You may just be a "positive-tester."

The implications are broad for people tested at random. For example, I was tested during a routine insurance exam, but because I have no risk factors, I had no concern about having AIDS. However, I was concerned about a "false positive," for which everyone has a risk. (In the 99 percent example, that risk is 20 out of 10,000.) Such a result might have made me uninsurable and destroyed both my personal and professional life. Fortunately, my test was negative. Anyone, however, might be one of those unlucky false positives, and that's the very serious risk of testing.

There's also the danger that "false-positive" people will feel they don't need to avoid sex with other "HIV-positive" people, a good route to infection that the "false-positive" people *don't* already have (the way they think they do).

But there's room for optimism in these statistics. An individual who is a random "positive" can find hope in them. This doesn't mean that he or she can take chances with other people's lives, of course, so each person must behave as though he or she is actually infected. But inwardly, the random HIV-positive individual has reason to be cautiously optimistic.

Of the many letters we received, here are a few excerpts:

Dear Marilyn:

As part of my Ph.D. dissertation research, I reviewed the then-existing accuracy (and the potential accuracy) of a wide range of medical diagnostic tests. I also modeled the accuracy that would be required before various classes of proposed tests could actually serve as reasonable, cost-effective aids to diagnosis.

Your column is the first publication that I have seen (in nearly forty years of looking) that provides a simple and an accurate explanation. I hope it helps educate the public and that it also helps educate medical researchers and medical care practitioners.

Howard Laitin, Ph.D.
Chief Scientist
Diversification and General Motors
Hughes Aircraft Company
El Segundo, California

I am glad that you brought this issue to light. Because these tests
are first tried on an affected-with-the-condition population sample, they
tend to be quite accurate and enthusiastically launched. However, when
tried in the general population, they produce a lot of false positive—and
quite unhappy—persons, as in the case of your drug-tested trucker.

George Dellaportas, M.D.
Clinton, South Carolina

Additional tests are arriving on the scene, and so I close on a hopeful note.
I wish this were the end of the subject. However, in the case of drug abuse,
and even more so in the case of AIDS, we all know it is not.

Part Four

Twenty-three

WISDOM AND KNOWLEDGE

Dear Marilyn:
Are people usually smarter than they think, or not as smart?

Sarah Mitchell
Dayton, Ohio

Dear Sarah:
It's been my personal experience that people are brighter than they think they are. I'm not sure why we usually undervalue ourselves, but one guess is that mass communication exposes us to so many experts these days that we feel brainless by comparison, forgetting that those experts are all separate people. Each often has spent his or her entire life learning about a special corner of the world (which is something any of us can do if we're inclined to), but knows no more than we do about anything else.

• • •

Dear Marilyn:
I'm a private investigator, and that helps a lot in looking at problems with a different attitude and viewpoint. Is there anything you could recommend to make me a better detective? "Observe and report" are our main responsibilities.

Patrick Lee Witeck
Costa Mesa, California

Dear Patrick:
It appears that "interpretation" is left to others, and while that may work very well for the way your company operates, taking "observe and report" too literally may make you less effective. The more you know about the situation, the more useful your observations will be to others.

I remember the first time I observed a cardiac surgery. Not knowing anything about the process, I would have been able to report only the most obvious procedures. But after I knew more, I could report what was *significant*. Next to studying, the best way I know to become a better "detective" in just about any field is to ask more questions.

●   ●   ●

Dear Marilyn:

Experts say we use only 5 percent to 10 percent of our brains. Is this true?

D. Bradley
Rock Island, Illinois

Dear Reader:

This is a popular notion, but I can't find any evidence to support it. I used to accept it myself, but I no longer do. Perhaps the idea comes from observing that people can recover with little permanent damage from even massive brain injuries. That's intriguing, but it's insufficient information to conclude that we only use a small portion of our brains. It also has been observed that people can die instantly from even the smallest injury to certain critical regions.

All in all, if you're wondering whether we might be using only a fraction of what we're capable of using, I believe the concept should be temporarily shelved. It's also possible that we use just about everything we've got, but that some areas are simply more important than others. At present, however, no one really knows.

●   ●   ●

Dear Marilyn:

A friend told me that if seven hundred monkeys were typing on seven hundred typewriters for seven hundred years, at least one of them would type a play by Shakespeare. Is this true? My friend says it is, but I disagree. Who is right?

Anonymous
Cuba, Illinois

Dear Reader:

You are; the odds against it are enormous. And this is an example of how much statements can become altered with repeated tellings. The original meant that if a monkey were typing for an infinite amount of time (with an infinite amount of time, we don't need an infinite number of monkeys), any result would be theoretically (and only theoretically) possible—including *Moby Dick*, *War and Peace*, and *Knitting With Dog Hair*.

●   ●   ●

Dear Marilyn:
    "Curiosity may have killed the cat, but it has also educated many a man." It appears that in the human race, the trait of curiosity has been more prominent in men than in women. Do you agree?

                                                        Archie Selders
                                                        Shelton, Washington

Dear Archie:
    Not at this time, I don't. I haven't yet discovered any evidence to suggest that women are any less inquisitive than men except that in the context of history, they have indeed been virtually absent from fields of invention and the like. But that simply may have been due to the fact that while men were busy developing new inventions, women were busy developing new inventors.

●   ●   ●

Dear Marilyn:
    How can a man who is very scholarly and possesses a tremendous amount of knowledge also be very absentminded? (Please, if you publish this, don't print my name. I don't want my husband to think I'm criticizing him— which, I guess, I am.)

                                                        Name Withheld
                                                        Duncan, Oklahoma

Dear Reader:
    I've noticed that only *men* are called absentminded! Like a tidy sock drawer, maybe absentmindedness is a luxury that a man can afford only if there's a devoted lady in the house.

●   ●   ●

Dear Marilyn:
    Do you agree, as some philosophers do, that there are no stupid questions—only stupid answers?

                                                        Connie Horvath
                                                        Palm Coast, Florida

Dear Connie:
    No. Please see the following question.

• • •

Dear Marilyn:
   Would you have been significantly more intelligent or marginally more intelligent had you been born a male?

F. Greg McGeary
Mount Pleasant, Pennsylvania

• • •

Dear Marilyn:
   If a statement is a fact, it's either right or wrong. But if it is not a fact, then your comment is an opinion—in which case, no one is right and no one is wrong. Nevertheless, why do some people feel that you are right or wrong, when an opinion is neither?

Mrs. Sammy Sigh
Crystal River, Florida

Dear Reader:
   Sometimes it's because so many of us have so many opinions about so many things about which we know very little that we sound silly to those who *do* know what they're talking about. In other words, we've strayed into areas of fact without realizing it. And this may apply even in fields such as art, which is generally considered wholly subjective. If an untraveled person said to me, "In my opinion, the works done by our local artists here in Hooterville are just as good as that stuff hanging in the Louvre," I'd probably tell him he was wrong.

• • •

Dear Marilyn:
   Would you rather be a member of a world-championship sports team or be a champion of an individual sport? And which sport would you choose?

B. B.
New Roads, Louisiana

Dear Reader:
   You've phrased your question to ask for a personal opinion, so I hope you don't mind getting just that. For a more physical sport, I'd like to be half of a winning pair of figure skaters, but for a more cerebral sport, I'd choose to win the world chess championship. While I think life's finest physical moments require partners, the greatest thinking has to be done alone.

•   •   •

Dear Marilyn:
Have you ever taken any psychedelic drugs? I took them when I was in college, and I remember feeling that if I were just a little smarter, I would have been able to grasp "the whole enchilada," and everything would have fallen into place.

Mike Ready
Universal City, Texas

Dear Mike:
No. For most of my younger years, I was far too busy trying to make a living and take care of my kids to have any time or motivation to experiment with drugs, which I think is just about the riskiest mental game anyone can play. The only "whole enchilada" I have ever tried to grasp was in a Mexican restaurant, and even *that* didn't work out too well.

•   •   •

Dear Marilyn:
We've all heard the gentle reminder, "Mind over matter." What does it really mean?

Dorothy Peterson
Susanville, California

Dear Dorothy:
In modern times, and to the more ambitious of us, it means, "Willpower alone can accomplish more than seems possible." But to the less ambitious of us, let's just leave it at this: "If nobody minds, it doesn't matter."

•   •   •

Dear Marilyn:
Is there anything less productive than wishful thinking?

R. L.
Chicago, Illinois

Dear Reader:
Oh gosh, yes. For one, I've noticed a phenomenon in which I walk past a carnival and think I smell cotton candy, when actually, after an extensive search, there turns out to be none. I call it "wishful smelling."

•   •   •

Dear Marilyn:
Which is greater, anticipation or realization?

George Simon
Fresno, California

Dear George:

It depends on whether you hope for the right stuff!

• • •

Dear Marilyn:

Would you say that the first step in anything is the most difficult?

Julian Hammer
Carteret, New Jersey

Dear Julian:

Sir, if only that were the case, we wouldn't have an overpopulation problem.

Twenty-four

CONDITION

Dear Marilyn:
    Do you believe when all is said and done that there is justice in the end?
I have a five-spot riding on it.

> Mike Miller
> Round Lake Park, Illinois

Dear Mike:
    No, I don't. And if you need proof, just spend a little time walking through
a hospital.

• • •

Dear Marilyn:
    I have had much joy and much sorrow in my life. I feel that I have been
to the extremes with each emotion! And yet, at the low periods—whether
they involved a loss of monetary means or a relationship that was dear to
me—I have been able to maintain peace and positiveness with my internal
assurance that "all things happen for a reason," and that in time these
reasons will become clear. Do you believe that there is any validity in such
a belief?

> Rose Pennington
> Lexington, Kentucky

Dear Rose:
    No. I don't think all bad things happen for a good reason ultimately, but
I doubt that this belief is what makes you so enviably stable. Plenty of
people who think likewise have given in and given up. In my own case, I
try to remind myself not to take anything too seriously for another reason—
remember, we're all biodegradable.

• • •

Dear Marilyn:

I've never paid much attention to all the stuff you hear about how you shouldn't smoke and you shouldn't drink and you shouldn't have a good time and all that. I think that if you're a good person, nothing really bad will happen to you (unless maybe you're real old, that is). What do you think?

Andy Wacker
Yankton, South Dakota

Dear Andy:

Remember, it was fun on the *Titanic* for a while, too.

• • •

Dear Marilyn:

Suppose there was a person who was intelligent enough to know that he was troubled with his life, but was unable to correct it. If there were a magical pill that would cure his problem by giving him total peace of mind regardless of his real-world experience, would you recommend he take it?

Dale Kurihara
Sanger, California

Dear Dale:

Assuming that you're not referring to situations such as the final phase of a terminal illness, for example, no, I would not. Even if people exist who *prefer* plant life to human life, there are far greater issues to be considered. Can you imagine the suffering such people could cause to others? Insensitive to consequences because they're content with any outcome, they would be free, depending upon their positions in life, to do everything from ruining their marriages to provoking wars.

• • •

Dear Marilyn:

While serving as a combat corpsman, I saw a slogan written on the back of a Marine's flack jacket: "For those who fight for it, life has a flavor the protected never know." I'll never forget this. Do you feel that a person must face death to appreciate life?

Bob Owens
Augusta, Georgia

Dear Bob:

It's great to see the positive attitude of that Marine, and I think the sentiment has true merit. Still, there are many flavors of appreciation, and

I don't feel a person must face death to gain one of them—I feel he must face life.

●   ●   ●

Dear Marilyn:
   Of these two strengths, human love and human reason, which is more powerful, and which is more important?
                                                                    Jenifer Marck
                                                                    Detroit, Michigan

Dear Jenifer:
   I think human love is more important, but human reason is more powerful. Love may give us some great intentions, but reason is what actually gets the job done.

●   ●   ●

Dear Marilyn:
   Is the saying, "Practice makes perfect" true? I don't think it is. For instance, in gym class during basketball, I never, *never* get the ball. Even if I practiced two hours every day for a month, I wouldn't be a good basketball player. Or for example, a girl takes piano. She hates it because she can't play her scales correctly. She tells her mother. But her mother says, "Practice makes perfect!" and continues to pay eight dollars a lesson.
                                                                    Mia Burns
                                                                    Temple Hills, Maryland

Dear Mia:
   You have my sympathy, dear. It has been my experience that practice alone doesn't make more than "pretty good."

●   ●   ●

Dear Marilyn:
   I can't remember names to save my soul! I just went back to school, and my grade point average was high, but I can forget the name of someone I've just met! I've tried to connect names with pictures or other words, but when I see the person, I'm not only searching for a name, I'm stuck for the "reminder," too. It's so embarrassing. Can this dimwit be saved?
                                                                    Jean Hanamoto
                                                                    Morgan Hill, California

Dear Jean:

Well, *this* dimwit sure doesn't know how. I've never been good at remembering names, either. But I've never found *anybody* who could remember them without really trying—probably because names are so capriciously given and almost entirely unrelated to the individual by virtue of logic or reason. Last names are even worse and often seem to be a bunch of syllables strung together like a social-security number. In other words, I'll bet you don't have a problem at all. I think forgetting names is perfectly normal.

● ● ●

Dear Marilyn:

Sometimes I want to put something away temporarily, but I always forget where I put it. Sometimes I find it weeks later. Maybe I'm getting old. Do you have a way to help me remember?

Vernon Mattingly
Flagstaff, Arizona

Dear Vernon:

Forget your age, Vernon. It happens to *everyone*. Here's a little trick I've used myself: Put the item away in a place that you use every day, but that no one else does. (Your desk drawer or your medicine cabinet, for example.) That way, if you forget where you put it, you'll find it within a day or two without even looking for it.

● ● ●

Dear Marilyn:

I was reading an article in a magazine about how women who "aren't so young anymore" should go through their closets and throw away certain articles of clothing because they actually make themselves look *older* (instead of younger) when they wear them. It prompted me to get rid of a few things. Afterward, though, I began to wonder what "not so young anymore" is. How can you tell if you are?

Georgette
Lawrenceville, Georgia

Dear Georgette:

If you read that article and got rid of a few things, you "aren't so young anymore."

● ● ●

Dear Marilyn:

I'll bet you can't give me a logical answer to the following question: Why do women wear pointed-toe shoes? Are they crazy? I've never seen a woman with pointed feet. (My dad is an engineer, and not even *he* can answer this question.)

Billy Jackson, Age 12
Denver, Colorado

Dear Billy:

Okay, I'll admit it's pretty crazy. But I'll bet you've never seen a man with a head shaped like a top hat, have you?

• • •

Dear Marilyn:

I'm a female who's six-feet-one-inch tall, and I can rarely go out in public without people asking a question about it. But the remarks I get when I answer are what bother me. Rarely does anyone believe me. They either say, "Oh, you're taller than that!" and give me a lecture on how I shouldn't be ashamed of my height, or they say something like, "Oh, you're not that tall! My son is six feet one, and you're not nearly as tall as he is!" I'd love to have something intelligent to say back. Can you help?

Karen Campbell
Smyrna, Tennessee

Dear Karen:

Have some fun. Tuck a dressmaker's tape into your handbag or coat pocket, and when people say something annoying like, "Oh no, you're not!" hand it over to them and reply, "How much do you want to bet?" (And if they have the guts to actually measure you, you'll at least make a little money!)

• • •

Dear Marilyn:

I am a girl, and I have spiked hair. Everybody that ever looks at me asks me if I am a girl or a boy, even when they *know* I'm a girl. Is there something smart I could say to them?

Karen Stabler
Dallas, Texas

Dear Karen:

Dear, I think the smartest thing you could say next time would be, "I think I'd better change my hairstyle."

• • •

Dear Marilyn:

Why are women never satisfied with their looks—even beautiful women?

Leetha Lundstrom-Wehner
Kailua-Kona, Hawaii

Dear Leetha:

It's cultural, not natural. Women have been trained to rely on looks far more than men do, which is why they wear makeup, too. But not all women are "never satisfied," and their number is growing. As women become more successful in more important areas, they grow less dependent on such embarrassingly trivial attributes as shapely eyebrows.

● ● ●

Dear Marilyn:

Sometimes I just feel bad about not being able to afford the better things I see for sale, and I wonder if there's something wrong with me that I can't afford them. The other day, I was looking at blankets, and they seemed so expensive. What do you think?

Laura Woody
Houston, Texas

Dear Laura:

I urge you to rethink your definition of "better"; it's not a synonym for expensive, and that's a sad mistake to make in life. If you're talking about a blanket, for example, it makes sense to call a warmer one or a softer one "better," but don't use that term to describe a fussier one or one whose only claim to fame is the citizenship of its sheep! Personally, I've walked into some of the "best" ladies clothing stores and walked right back out, almost laughing. Both the prices *and* the clothes were a joke!

Twenty-five

Dear Marilyn

Why does society still cling to the stereotype of girl babies wearing pink and boy babies wearing blue?

Janet Baier
Williamsport, Pennsylvania

Dear Janet:

So well-meaning people (like me) would not lean over carriages and say, "What a pleasant-tempered baby you have. How old is it?"

● ● ●

Dear Marilyn:

Why are children referred to as "kids"? Whenever I hear it, the first thing that comes into my mind is a bunch of goats.

Mary Gallos
Fairfield, Connecticut

Dear Mary:

Me, too. Using "kids," which is what the young of the goat are called, in reference to human children is a term of affection that refers to the playful "frisky" qualities goats and children share. We can just as well, and sometimes do, call them "lambs," referring to their sweet, docile natures. That's why we call them "kids" so much more often!

● ● ●

Dear Marilyn:

I'm a teenager, and my grandfather is in his seventies, and he sure reminisces a lot. Why do grandparents do that so much? I don't.

Brian Fellers
Knoxville, Tennessee

Dear Brian:
I hope you're not too jealous, but it's just that older folks have so much more to reminisce *about* than you do.

●   ●   ●

Dear Marilyn:
Since college, I have noticed my ability to concentrate decline. Any suggestions on how to improve it?

Michael Sanders
Lenexa, Kansas

Dear Michael:
Go to a bookstore and treat yourself to a novel, but not one that's a classic or that you think you "should" read. Instead, ask a few people for advice, by inquiring, "Read any good novels lately? I'm looking for a recommendation," and then spend a leisurely hour reading jackets and browsing. (And don't turn to nonfiction; learning about a subject is too much of a chore, and a storyline can make turning the pages a pleasure.) When you return to reading, other old abilities return, too.

●   ●   ●

Dear Marilyn:
I'm in my middle forties now, and my outlook on life and approach to everyday living is very different from when I was in my twenties. My friends feel the same way, but none of us knows how to sum it up. Can you?

Barbara Krakower
Spring Hill, Florida

Dear Barbara:
Forty is the age when you start trading your psychological problems for physical ones.

●   ●   ●

Dear Marilyn:
What does it mean when people say, "I have to go find myself"? I'm in my sixties, and when I was young, no one ever said that. We were never lost. I know where I am, and I know who I am. Have I missed something?

Mary Ann
Columbia, Illinois

Dear Mary Ann:
I think "finding one's self" has nothing to do with feeling lost. Rather, it refers to an attempt to get away from the pressures of "home" and take a

little time to see what kind of people we are or could become, independent of our upbringing or our current circumstances. It can be an uplifting experience, and I'd certainly recommend it to the young at heart. And forget your age, Mary Ann. You're not gone—this *is* your day!

● ● ●

Dear Marilyn:

Why do some people think that you have "lost it" after you reach the age of seventy or so? I'm past seventy, and I feel that I will never get too old to learn.

Vivian Renetta Gifford
Fort Worth, Texas

Dear Vivian:

Older folks are often victims of stereotyping just the way other age groups are. Treating them as though they're all alike is as senseless as treating teenagers as though they're all alike. A few young people are troublemakers, but the rest are just fine, and a few senior citizens have "lost it," all right, but the rest of them have it locked up tight, and it's drawing interest, too!

● ● ●

Dear Marilyn:

As I approach my mid-seventies, I often wonder what causes me to perceive younger people as so young. Of course, this doesn't apply to children, but rather to the group of people aged thirty to fifty or so, for example. I often find myself looking at senators and congressmen and saying to myself, "What are those youngsters doing running the country?" What do you think causes this perception?

Milton Grubman
Fair Lawn, New Jersey

Dear Milton:

I think you're now seeing things as they actually are! When we're very young and have little experience in life, we form the mistaken impression that people over the age of thirty or forty are vastly knowledgeable, which we later discover isn't true at all. But first impressions die hard.

● ● ●

Dear Marilyn:

I'm in my late-seventies now, and I'm often conscious of having dreamed when I wake up, but I usually can't remember what it was about. Is the inability to remember dreams another sign of advancing age?

Dorothy McCamman
Washington, D.C.

Dear Dorothy:

No, and considering the kinds of dreams *I* often have, I'd call it plain old good luck.

● ● ●

Dear Marilyn:

Please settle a difference of opinion between me and the missus. Now celebrating our "golden years," we find ourselves at odds over the issue of whether older people have the capacity to learn new things. Many years ago, the missus began playing the accordion, but to this day she knows virtually one song—"Lady of Spain." Each time I urge her to take lessons and learn other songs, she says, "Old dogs can't learn new tricks." To which I say, "Pish, tosh, woman," which results in her reply—another spirited chorus of "Lady of Spain." I recently learned how to play the tuba. Don't my "oompah-pahs" bear me out?

> J. B.
> Wantagh, New York

Dear Reader:

I think they do. And I sympathize with you, too. I had a relative who played the "Beer Barrel Polka" on his accordion (and *only* the "Beer Barrel Polka"). You can tell the missus that my last old dog learned how to untie my shoelaces without slobbering all over them at an advanced age, so she has no excuse. (But don't expect too much of her; my dog would walk through the hula hoop just fine, but I never could get him to jump.)

● ● ●

Dear Marilyn:

When does one really become a "senior citizen"?

> E. Engelhardt
> Warminster, Pennsylvania

Dear Reader:

When one finally realizes that he no longer just *thinks* he knows more than most younger folks—he actually *does*.

Twenty-six

ON HUMAN
NATURE

Dear Marilyn:
　　You are in a lifeboat from a luxury yacht that just sank. The boat is overloaded with a dozen people. Some *must* be put overboard; otherwise, you all will be swamped in the next wave and drown. You are elected to determine who stays and who goes. Excluding a blind lottery (like drawing straws), how do you determine human worth as to who stays or swims? Would it be according to age? Intelligence? Physical fitness? Or some other factor?

Tom Filippone
Basking Ridge, New Jersey

Dear Tom:
　　I'd first ask for volunteers to leave the lifeboat. Let's say only two or three especially kindhearted people offer. I'd then designate those people to *remain*, not go. Next, out of the remaining group, I'd ask for volunteers again. Let's say half a dozen of them now offer to leave. I'd take them up on it. That way, in addition to handling the situation with volunteers, we'd at least be left with the good and the honest.

● ● ●

Dear Marilyn:
　　Why does it always seem to be that good things happen for bad people and that bad things happen to good people?

Dennis Oshiro
Honolulu, Hawaii

Dear Dennis:
　　I don't think they do! Rather, this is just the stuff that we notice most because it makes us all so darned mad.

• • •

Dear Marilyn:
Briefly, what do you think is the "root of all evil"?

Frank Wulczynski
Elizabeth, Pennsylvania

Dear Frank:
"Ignorance."

• • •

Dear Marilyn:
When I grew up, I was taught that it was *good* to be a discriminating person. Why does the word also mean something bad?

Hilly Jones-Bangert
Knoxville, Tennessee

Dear Hilly:
Because there's a difference between discriminating *among* and discriminating *against*.

• • •

Dear Marilyn:
What do you think of a company that would take advantage of a loophole in the zoning laws and plop its corporate headquarters right smack in the middle of the only nice lake view in town?

Albert Ross
City Withheld

Dear Albert:
It sounds like the corporate *hindquarters* to me.

• • •

Dear Marilyn:
I've heard there are two kinds of people—"doers" and "thinkers." What do *you* think?

Greg Murphy
Ridgewood, New Jersey

Dear Greg:
It depends on my mood. When I'm not in as good a mood as usual, I think there are two kinds of people in this world, all right: "doers" and "those they do it to."

• • •

Dear Marilyn:
  Why are people's words and deeds so often different?
                                                    N. Katz
                                                    West Palm Beach, Florida

Dear Reader:
  Because people think best in private, but behave best in public.

• • •

Dear Marilyn:
  Which is worse: to trust everyone or not to trust *anyone*?
                                                    Jill Brady
                                                    Cochranton, Pennsylvania

Dear Jill:
  It has been my experience that the more we trust people, the more they live up to our trust—so trusting everyone tends to let us live our lives in far better company.

• • •

Dear Marilyn:
  Why is it that a person can control his physical actions but cannot control his thoughts with the same degree of success? If I don't want to do something like overeat or overdrink, for example, I usually can stop myself. But if I don't want to upset myself with negative ideas, I don't seem to have the same degree of control.
                                                    Anonymous
                                                    Grand Rapids, Michigan

Dear Reader:
  I know what you mean—but I'll bet you *do* have just about the same degree of control. Take that temptation to order a rich dessert, for example. That was a thought, not an action. But you didn't prevent it from popping up after dinner, did you? Or how about the desire to stay in bed after your alarm rings in the morning? In other words, *all* those things you mention are thoughts, not just some of them. So maybe you're just noticing the thoughts that you don't "turn down" the way you do a thought that suggests another drink.

• • •

Dear Marilyn:
  I hear a lot about "type A" and "type B" personalities, but can you give me a quick way to tell which one I am?
                                                    Olivia Reed
                                                    Leland, Mississippi

Dear Olivia:

Yes. If you're a "type B" personality, you'll be satisfied with this answer; if you're a "type A" personality, you'll feel like hitting me over the head with a sack of mail.

•   •   •

Dear Marilyn:

What makes a person an expert?

Robert Gentry
Haubstadt, Indiana

Dear Robert:

A person is an expert in a subject when he not only knows everything you can learn about it, he also knows which of that stuff is wrong.

•   •   •

Dear Marilyn:

On a recent trip, my husband took a wrong turn, and we drove around for an hour not knowing where we would end up, as there were few road signs. I say we were lost, but my husband doesn't agree. Are you lost when you don't know where you are? (P.S. A man will *never* admit he is lost!)

M. L. Barnes
Spokane, Washington

Dear Reader:

For the most part, I believe that you aren't lost until you need help. That is, there could be two people in the same spot, neither knowing exactly where they are, but with one of them lost and the other not. And this may be why certain people are loath to stop and ask directions!

•   •   •

Dear Marilyn:

Why is it that in the animal world, the male is usually more colorful than the female and uses its colors to attract females, but among humans, just the opposite is the case? Male peacocks, for example, spread their gorgeous tails to attract females, who are plain by comparison, but female humans paint their faces and wear colorful clothing to attract males.

Sandra Gordon
Greensboro, North Carolina

Dear Sandra:

These situations aren't analogous. Female humans aren't any more colorful naturally than male humans, and the "attractive" behaviors they exhibit are entirely cultural, although they've certainly become a long-standing habit. But plenty of people, both male and female, dislike the whole notion of makeup intensely. Back in 1770, a bill was introduced into the English Parliament that read, "That all women . . . that shall . . . seduce, and betray into matrimony, any of His Majesty's subjects, by scents, paints, cosmetic washes, artificial teeth, false hair, Spanish wool, iron stays, hoops, high heeled shoes, [or] bolstered hips, shall incur the penalty of the law in force against witchcraft . . . and that the marriage, upon conviction, shall stand null and void." (The early Colonists also disliked cosmetics, and this bill was actually adopted in Pennsylvania.) Sounds like it was written by a fellow who'd been burned *himself* once too often, doesn't it?!

● ● ●

Dear Marilyn:

Do you agree with the following comment? "The reason that the all-American boy prefers beauty to brains is that he can see better than he can think."

Charles Check
Plano, Texas

Dear Charles:

For boys, yes. But for *men*, no.

● ● ●

Dear Marilyn:

My father says he is "18 reversed." It sounds like he wants to be a teenager again. Should my mother be jealous if he starts looking at good-looking women?

L. F.
Seattle, Washington

Dear Reader:

No. If he's 81, she should be *happy*.

● ● ●

Dear Marilyn:

Why do people who have gorgeous, naturally curly hair say such irritating things when you compliment them? Like, "Oh, it's so much trouble to take care of," or "I'm tired of it." It makes you want to strangle them.

Georgette Mink
Kailua-Kona, Hawaii

Dear Georgette:
Maybe they're just being truthful and modest. After all, how would you like to hear, "Why, thanks! It's not always easy to handle, but I do look gorgeous most of the time, don't I?"

●   ●   ●

Dear Marilyn:
Why is it that women with blond hair are considered lightweights? Genetically, is there any validity to this?

H. K.
Rogers City, Michigan

Dear Reader:
Genetically speaking, natural blondes are no more or less serious than natural brunettes. However, few of the blondes you see in this country are those natural ones, and our culture discriminates against people who bleach their hair, whether female *or* male. It's regarded as frivolous behavior, much the same as wearing makeup, and the person usually suffers some loss of credibility, whether deserved or not.

●   ●   ●

Dear Marilyn:
I recently read that a poll of college students showed that they're interested first in sex, second in food, and third in work. What a sad commentary. Do you think that's really true of most of them? You know how those surveys are.

Violet Biffel
Houston, Texas

Dear Violet:
No, I *don't* think it's true. I think most of them are *far* more interested in work than in food.

●   ●   ●

Dear Marilyn:
Is normal life full of sex, money, pride, and greed?

Julian Hammer
Carteret, New Jersey

Dear Julian:
Only if you handle it right.

Twenty-seven

Dear Marilyn:
 When a friendship fades, how do you say goodbye?
 Mrs. Avis Burrows
 Saint Albans, West Virginia

Dear Reader:
 You should never say goodbye to a friend. Remember, friends are a lot harder to get than relatives.

● ● ●

Dear Marilyn:
 Should I try to find a mate with comparable intelligence?
 Andrew Griffin
 Hoboken, Georgia

Dear Andrew:
 "Comparable" may be fine for professional relationships, but I think "compatible" works far better for personal ones. I know plenty of bright people, but there are very few of them I want to see looking back at me over the breakfast table.

● ● ●

Dear Marilyn:
 How can you tell if a person is going to be compatible?
 Harold Wampler
 East Islip, New York

Dear Harold:

When you meet someone you feel like you've known all your life, you know you've met a friend.

•   •   •

Dear Marilyn:

A friend told me about a line from a poem or a play that says that when truth and kindness conflict, one ought to choose kindness in interpersonal communications. Do you know of it?

B. A. McDonald
Peru, New York

Dear Reader:

No, but I can offer you one of my own: In every relationship, there are times when a little honesty is better than a lot.

•   •   •

Dear Marilyn:

Why do women give abusive men another chance to become nicer, but they don't give men who they think are too nice (and whom they commonly refer to as "wimps") another chance to become meaner?

Leo Ortiz
Mesa, Arizona

Dear Leo:

You've got *me*; I wouldn't give either *one* of them another chance.

•   •   •

Dear Marilyn:

Can you give me just one good reason why I shouldn't look for an attractive woman to marry rather than an ordinary one?

Don Rinder
Richardson, Texas

Dear Don:

Unless you're very suggestible, Don, a good-looking set of china won't make the meal taste any better.

I knew I'd get a significant amount of "pro" and "con" mail regarding this response, but I'd expected the "pro" to be from women and the "con" to be from men. Instead, it was just the reverse. See the following column we published in reply.

Dear Marilyn:
    I am fuming over your answer because I am a very attractive woman searching for someone to marry. What is wrong with looking for good looks and *then* finding out what is inside? I pray no males read your column this week!

Sharon Hoffert
West Lawn, Pennsylvania

    I agree that when the lights are out, looks don't mean a thing, but some men want a pretty woman to wake up to in the morning. I am glad I have beauty, a trim figure, and brains to offer a man. Beautiful women can be faithful, loving, smart, and in need of being held all night for the rest of their lives just like low cheek-boned broads!

Marietta Wilhelm
Eugene, Oregon

Dear Readers:
    Of course they can. Which is why such women should have more than a guy who just wants a pretty woman to wake up to in the morning. After all, when that pretty woman loses her looks with time, she doesn't want the sort of man who will then leave her for another woman who's still pretty, does she?

Dear Marilyn:
    I got rid of the china, and I kept the stoneware.

Deborah Wright
Roanoke, Virginia

• • •

Dear Marilyn:
    I have a friend who still thinks he can find his true love. The thing is that his requirements are impossible. He's a tall, good-looking, intelligent, never-married, and chaste vegetarian in his late thirties. He's looking for a tall, good-looking, intelligent, never-married, and chaste vegetarian woman in her thirties. I'm afraid he'll never marry. I've tried to explain to him that the odds of finding such a woman are infinitesimally small. What do *you* think?

Montana Rae
Martinsburg, West Virginia

Dear Montana:
I think the guy's *already* found his true love: *himself.*

●   ●   ●

Dear Marilyn:
Why do men and women choose to meet each other through correspondence? (I have met women this way, but I also meet them in other ways.) Is there a reason for this?

George Coffin
Kahoka, Missouri

Dear George:
Well, "hope" might be a pretty good one. When you read through a page of ads, your heart leaps at the prospect of meeting any of those dazzling paragons of sex appeal, respectability, and success, and you can have *days* of glorious anticipation before discovering the real person behind the print. (And how would you meet this person otherwise, anyway?) But if you walked into an office party with all those same people standing around, you'd be far less impressed.

●   ●   ●

Dear Marilyn:
I recently ran into the man I almost married in the sixties. He said that the reason we didn't get to the altar was that he loved me "too much." I think that it is impossible for a human being to experience *any* emotion "too much." What do you think?

S. K. L.
Wayne, New Jersey

Dear Reader:
I think that the shell-shocked soldier, the manic, and the suicidal person, among others, would disagree. (Not that your ex-boyfriend is emotionally ill, of course; perhaps his complaint is simply a case of "warm heart, cold feet.")

●   ●   ●

Dear Marilyn:
I recently read that a single man's lifespan is years less than a married man's, but they didn't say why. Do you know?

J. W. Scott, Jr.
Baltimore, Maryland

Dear Reader:
    No, I don't. Even though the death rate for single men is twice as high as for married men, and the death rate for single women is one and a half times as high as for married women, it simply may be that people who are less healthy are less likely to marry and that numerous other factors are involved. I certainly wouldn't jump to the conclusion that marriage is a sort of haven from stress!

● ● ●

Dear Marilyn:
    I was married for a decade and have been divorced for two decades. I seem to be much happier divorced. Am I fooling myself and rationalizing my single state? Is true happiness possible for people who don't have a romantic interest in their lives?

Anonymous
Fargo, North Dakota

Dear Reader:
    Ah, but you're talking to a woman for whom a long walk in the woods is a romantic experience. My best guess is "yes." Not only do I know plenty of single people who appear happy, I also know plenty of happily married people who appear to have no romantic interest in their lives whatsoever!

● ● ●

Dear Marilyn:
    How come women who can't sew, can admit it and laugh? But if a woman admits she can't cook, she's looked upon with scorn.

Mrs. Del De Mage
Magnolia, Mississippi

Dear Reader:
    Sounds like a comment about men, not women. And if that's the case, you're just saying that most men would rather eat than wear clothes!

● ● ●

Dear Marilyn:
    Can you give me a good reply to a man who says, "Woman's only purpose on this Earth is to serve man"?

Ann Ewing Baird
Lake Havasu City, Arizona

Dear Ann:

"Goodbye" sums up my thoughts nicely.

A number of women readers wrote with alternate suggestions, some of them unprintable, but the most common went something like this: "Woman's only purpose on this Earth is to serve man—on a bed of rice with fresh vegetables"!

● ● ●

Dear Marilyn:

How can a couple—either husband and wife or boyfriend and girlfriend— be so in love for years and then one or the other end the relationship as if nothing happened or it doesn't bother them. I don't understand, and I've seen it happen lots of times, including to me.

Karen
Newark, New Jersey

Dear Karen:

I'm not an expert in affairs of the heart, but I think your own words "as if" are the answer. No one leaves a long-term love relationship without pain, but some people are stoic enough not to show it.

● ● ●

Dear Marilyn:

We have murder, rape, child abuse, divorce, and so on, yet we have no courses in our junior and senior high schools on human relations, specifically, marriage and child-rearing. Why?

Bert Maupin
Anchorage, Alaska

Dear Bert:

If we really don't have enough of such courses, maybe it's because we really don't know how to do them right. Personally, I think anyone who has the nerve to teach a course on either of those particular subjects should have a virtually flawless marriage and/or virtually flawless children. (And both the marriage *and* the kids have to be at least twenty-five years old.)

● ● ●

Dear Marilyn:

How can several children—same parents, two or three years apart in age, growing up in the same home environment with similar experiences—grow up to be so completely different?

Lori Rust Haberkern
King, North Carolina

Dear Lori:

Aside from all the other factors, they're made out of completely different stuff. Contrary to common belief, children resulting from a particular female/male relationship are not half "the mother" and half "the father." If they were, they would all look alike. Instead, they come half from the mother's *entire inheritable gene pool* and half from the father's *entire inheritable gene pool*, and each individual combination is wildly haphazard. This gives siblings far less in common than we've historically believed, not just with each other, but with their parents, as well. One mating has the capability of producing many trillions of genetically different offspring.

●   ●   ●

Dear Marilyn:

I've been trying to find out for years if there is an "only child" support group. Do you know if there is one?

A. Fox
Kenosha, Wisconsin

Dear Reader:

No, but since when do kids need group therapy just because they don't have siblings? It's not always easy to be the only child in a family, but neither is it always easy to have an older sister or younger brother, or be the only girl or the only boy, or be the youngest or the one in the middle or the oldest—or be a parent, for that matter. Why not join a bridge club or a hiking club or a charitable organization instead and focus on something a little more constructive?

●   ●   ●

Dear Marilyn:

The daughter of a friend is a straight-A college student who lives at home. After she bought a car with her savings, her father set a 12:30 A.M. curfew, explaining that he wanted her home before the bars closed at 1:00 A.M. to avoid drunks on the highway. The daughter argued that it didn't matter because "if her time was up, then her time was up." The father relented. Who's correct? I think the daughter is ignoring the law of probabilities to serve her own end.

Harry Decker
Phoenix, Arizona

Dear Harry:

Dad was had. The same faulty logic would justify her taking up bronco-busting, drag-racing, or skydiving—without a parachute.

•   •   •

Dear Marilyn:

Why is it that the people we love the most as children—our parents—are the same people we want around the least when we are adults?

Sally Bennett
South Lake Tahoe, California

Dear Sally:

I think the answer depends on the parents and the children themselves. Parents who continue to treat grown children like "kids" are seldom welcome. And even those parents who don't do that, may have grown children who are insecure enough to feel that way, anyway. Worse, grown children may unconsciously revert to childhood behavior patterns around their parents, creating a problem that might not even exist otherwise. It's a tough issue, and I certainly don't know how to resolve it. In my own case, I just got lucky, I guess. The older my mother and I get, the more I seem to like her.

Twenty-eight

Dear Marilyn:
Do you think that love is greater than gravity?

Sue Joe
Greenwood, Mississippi

Dear Sue:
Hmmm. Well, gravity is feeble compared to magnetism, and dogs' noses behave like little black magnets, all right; whenever they get near each other, they touch.

● ● ●

Dear Marilyn:
Is there any reality to the phenomenon of "true love at first sight"? I'm speaking of the type of love that lives on and on—not just a passing infatuation.

Annie Rachel
San Diego, California

Dear Annie:
Sure—and another word for it is "coincidence." Out of all the people in the world and all those garden-variety episodes of sexual attraction, there are bound to be a few of us who are lucky enough to have it happen with someone who keeps our interest up more than our dander.

● ● ●

Dear Marilyn:
Do we love with our hearts? What happens when a heart is transplanted to another person?

M. P. V.
Tucson, Arizona

Dear Reader:

I'm involved in cardiovascular research, have personally witnessed cardiac surgeries, and I can assure you that the heart is little more than a beautiful pump. Emotions arise from the brain, which means that love is "all in your head."

I received two complaints about that reply, both from people who insisted that the heart is more than just "a beautiful pump." I can understand this sentiment, but they then went on to relate the following story: In the words of one, "There have been televised news stories in which recipients of heart transplants have suddenly adopted the behavior of the person from whom they received the heart, even though the donor was unknown to them. One middle-aged woman, who did not frequent fast-food places, developed an urge to consume Chicken McNuggets, which she had never eaten. The young man whose heart she had received had been riding a motorcycle at the time of his death and was carrying a box of Chicken McNuggets, his favorite food." I wonder if she took up riding a motorcycle, too! (This sounds like the beginning of another great urban myth to me.)

● ● ●

Dear Marilyn:

If you had to choose to spend the rest of your life with someone you were in love with or someone who was in love with you (but not vice versa in either case), which would you choose?

Rhae Nell Ahlstrom-Ward
Atlanta, Georgia

Dear Rhae:

Hmmm. I suspect that as I grow older and older, the people who are in love with me will look better and better.

● ● ●

Dear Marilyn:

Why does love hurt so bad when it's gone?

John Burnett
Peoria, Illinois

Dear John:

It doesn't. It only hurts when it's *still there.*

● ● ●

Dear Marilyn:

What's the difference between a broken heart and a broken spirit?

H. C.
Bridgeport, Connecticut

Dear Reader:
   To me, the major difference between a broken heart and a broken spirit is that people break hearts and time mends them, but *time* breaks spirits and *people* mend them.

●   ●   ●

Dear Marilyn:
   Isn't it true that love and crying are always selfish? Love has a selfish motive—a need, a gratification, or security—and crying is self-pity, either directly or indirectly.

Bruno Tambellini
Pittsburgh, Pennsylvania

Dear Bruno:
   Although some of it probably *is* selfish, I'm sure it's not always that way. But what if it were? What's so bad about self-fulfilling behavior that it should be so roundly denigrated as "selfish"? Is eating selfish? Is supporting ourselves selfish? Or do you think we should only feed and support *others* while those others feed and support *us*?

●   ●   ●

Dear Marilyn:
   How can a person be truly happy without closing his or her eyes to the problems facing mankind?

S. Bobo
Arlington, Texas

Dear Reader:
   When has there been a time in history when humankind faced no serious problems? In other words, you imply that no one who has ever lived should be happy! How about opening our eyes to all the good, instead? Why not identify with all the joy in the world instead of all the suffering? Happy people are perfectly capable of having compassion for others. If you want to spend your life lamenting the whims of nature and the sins of humankind, that's your business. But be aware that you may be wasting precious time in a life that's already very short.

●   ●   ●

Dear Marilyn:
   What is your thinking about the notion that happiness is obtained only by doing things yourself and not through someone else's accomplishments?

Lois Van Horn
San Diego, California

Dear Lois:

I think that it depends on how much you had to do with that other person's accomplishments. As far as I'm concerned, a physical therapist has every right to be delighted when she sees her stroke patient take his first halting step down the hall.

• • •

Dear Marilyn:

My favorite quote of yours is, "I think any life is worthwhile that produces more than it consumes, whether it's handbooks, harmonicas, or happiness." I've used it several times in defense against persistent ridicule by family members. My own little sister called me "a middle-aged creep." Do you think it's wrong to justify one's social shortcomings or lack of professional success with such a quote, or do you think I'm hiding behind philosophy?

Joe
Denver, Colorado

Dear Joe:

Don't be so hard on yourself, Joe. We all have social shortcomings, only a few of us have worldly success, and *none* of us should listen to people who make us feel lousy about it.

• • •

Dear Marilyn:

Would you agree that nobody can give real happiness to others unless he or she is first truly happy with themselves?

Jack O'Hanlon
Tucson, Arizona

Dear Jack:

No, I wouldn't. As an extreme example, just consider all those people who have committed suicide. Surely many of them had given real happiness to others, but they were extremely unhappy with their *own* lives.

After that reply was published, I received quite a few letters. Here are some excerpts:

Dear Marilyn:

Your answer was a lovely note of grace that touched me and, I hope, a great many others. In 1988, I lost my only son to suicide at the age of sixteen. I have found it very sad that so many of Anthony's friends and even family have been unable or unwilling to remember the many, many moments of happiness he had brought to others. I hope that others reading your reply were as touched as I am and come to realize that a victim of suicide can be remembered for the many kinds of goodness they gave us and not the awful way they left us. My son was never a saint, but he was a son that I always will be proud of. You wrote only one sentence, but it was beautiful. Anthony left quite a legacy, and perhaps we can focus on that legacy now.

Betty Adams
Annapolis, Maryland

I want to thank you very much for your answer to the question regarding happiness. You were correct in my case. For four years, my fiancé and I were very happy. Jack was the most loving, giving, sensitive person I had ever met. He showed me the true joys of love and life. But he himself was not happy. Finally, he reached the end of his rope and committed suicide. It's been difficult to pick up the pieces and get on without him. For the first couple of years, all I could remember was his death, but now I can remember his life. Thank you again for your insight. You're correct. It does not take a happy person to make someone else happy.

Terri Stamey
Smyrna, Georgia

This is my first letter to a newspaper. If you are never right again, I believe even you cannot imagine how many people you made happy with your answer.

Emma Walker
Washington, D. C.

What beautiful letters. And the people who wrote them are even more beautiful. They are living proof of the love that was left to them by the dear ones who are now gone, and they can take comfort in the knowledge that their loved ones undoubtedly would be proud of them, too. I know I am.

Twenty-nine

MORALS AND
ETHICS

Dear Marilyn:

What is better for mankind—people who *won't* break the rules or people who *will* break the rules?

Ann Haas
Camp Hill, Pennsylvania

Dear Ann:

It depends on the sort of people they are (and which rules you have in mind!). If people are greedy, it's better if they don't break the rules. But if they're generous, it often can be better if they do.

● ● ●

Dear Marilyn:

As a longtime elementary-school teacher, I have assured children that "honesty is the best policy" while watching small miscreants deny responsibility. I was jostled by children in a cathedral in Europe and lost three hundred dollars to small fingers. Dishonesty does pay well; denial gives the doer a chance to escape. Can you present an argument that might justify honesty to the ambivalent young?

Edith Battles
Redondo Beach, California

Dear Edith:

Here's something you can tell the kids. Honesty is the best policy for the *wrongdoer*, not for his or her victim, and this is why: When misdeeds are used to achieve a goal, the offender is actually learning incompetent behavior. It's far easier to earn a dollar than it is to steal a dollar because society is dead set against dishonesty, and the person who attempts to use it will find himself or herself thwarted at every turn. Moreover, the admission of wrongdoing is a step in the right direction; it shows you have courage, and it shows you repudiate unprincipled behavior. And most important, it shows that to *you*.

●   ●   ●

Dear Marilyn:
    We're having a heated argument in my office over being asked to lie. When your boss (who signs your paycheck, by the way) approaches you to lie for him, do you share in the blame for telling that lie, or is he alone responsible for it? I'm the only one who says that it's his lie and that I'm just following orders. I would appreciate your reasoning in this matter.

                                                        A. W.
                                                        Albany, New York

Dear Reader:
    Ethical behavior should not be relegated to the status of a weekend activity, and if more people knew that, especially in government, this would be a better world.
    You share in the culpability because you're not chained to your desk. That is, you have a choice. However, whether you exercise that choice will be directly proportionate to the importance of the lie and the importance of retaining your job, and people will understand that. This is the crux of the matter, and it can't be dismissed with a black-and-white code of ethics. You have to think about it.
    Suppose you feel that the truth must be told at all times. A stranger appears in the office with a deadly weapon and says she's going to kill your boss. Your boss asks you to tell her he's left for the day. Should you show her in, instead?
    Or let's say you feel that following orders absolves one of personal responsibility, and your boss asks you to shift all funds from the company retirement account to his personal checking account in South America and make sure his passport is up to date. Should you do it?
    In the unlikely event that your boss asks you to do something of which you should be ashamed, you should decline with as much grace as possible. This is indeed taking a risk, but it's equally unlikely that you'll be dismissed as a result.

• • •

Dear Marilyn:
   While under the influence of alcohol or drugs, many people embarrass themselves, behave badly, and even commit brutal crimes. As these substances partly (or completely) remove the control that people more normally exercise over their actions—and the actions without the control are reprehensible—does this mean that many people are inherently bad?

Frank Pipal
Teaneck, New Jersey

Dear Frank:
   No—not unless you think the unrestrained behavior of the rest of the animal kingdom is bad. Life is brutal for fireflies, hummingbirds, and pandas alike, and it would be the same for us if we didn't exercise a little control over our animal natures. Have you ever seen ads for products that promise to "bring out the animal in you"? Well, I'd rather keep the cage door shut, thanks.

• • •

Dear Marilyn:
   Driving is usually a normal activity for me. On the city streets, I can be passed by a car and not pay any attention, yet being passed on the highway is totally different. I feel that I must pass everyone in sight and never be passed by other drivers, completely disregarding the speed limit and possible dangers. Would you consider this competitiveness, insecurity, a type of revenge, or merely human nature?

Name Withheld
Casper, Wyoming

Dear Reader:
   I believe you're asking this question because you suspect you have a problem, but you hope that you don't. The answer to why you feel you must pass everyone on the highway may be a combination of all those things you mention—but it doesn't matter. You're violating society's rules just as much as if you were to steal money from a cash register or punch someone you didn't like, even though it may be only human nature to want to.
   But I respect you for noticing this weakness in yourself, which is difficult to admit. Ask your family doctor to refer you to someone from whom you can get professional help, and in the meantime, please be compassionate and stay off the highway.

• • •

Dear Marilyn:
World peace is a subject much talked about. History shows that many, if not most, wars were instituted by religions proclaiming, "Ours is the only true faith." True or false—There will never be world peace as long as there are churches.

Vyrl Owens
Kaleva, Michigan

Dear Vyrl:
I understand your point, but I think you've gone too far. Although the behavior of the various religious faiths has not always been exemplary, I'm inclined to think that any religion that honestly preaches peace is far more likely to be a positive force than a negative force in that regard.

• • •

Dear Marilyn:
Let's say two universes exist—one in which God does not exist, but the beings there believe He does, the other in which God does exist, but no one there believes He does. Which universe would be the best place to live?

Richard Pratt
Sparks, Nevada

Dear Richard:
I'd rather live in the second world—but not for too long!

• • •

Dear Marilyn:
My class has just finished learning about mythology. Almost all the gods in mythology are immortal, so why are some young-looking and some old-looking? When do immortals stop aging?

Susan Jeroslow
Austin, Texas

Dear Susan:
Because myths are intended to instruct, most of the gods and goddesses stop aging at the point when they are at the height of the power (or quality) that they are meant to represent. Gods of strength, for example, look younger; goddesses of wisdom look older.

• • •

Dear Marilyn:

Some great thinkers say God created man, and other great thinkers say man created God. What is the minimalist worst-case scenario for afterlife between these two extremes?

John Verde
Akron, Ohio

Dear John:

There'll be a heaven, but you won't be able to find a parking space.

Thirty

Dear Marilyn:
   Could you tell me if there are any reputable astrologers in the Dallas-Fort Worth area?

L. L. Shipley
Rockwall, Texas

Dear Reader:
   Yes, I can, and no, there aren't. (And I would have said the same thing no matter *where* you lived.)

● ● ●

Dear Marilyn:
   Is there any validity to numerology, or is it designed to part the gullible from their money? I'd like to know your opinion before spending time and money on it.

R. M. Kane
San Francisco, California

Dear Reader:
   Numerology is pure nonsense. And that's not an opinion—that's a fact.

● ● ●

Dear Marilyn:
   Why in this day and age do we still not label the thirteenth floor as such in many tall buildings? Where did this all begin?

Fred Walter
Fort Lee, New Jersey

Dear Fred:
No one knows, but there are all sorts of folklore guesses ranging from thirteen people (Judas being the thirteenth) at the Last Supper and the Crucifixion taking place on Friday the thirteenth, to Norse myth and even witchcraft. But I'm sure you could find just as many things about the number twelve—or any other number, for that matter. This "unlucky number" business is all a lot of hooey.

• • •

Dear Marilyn:
Do you believe in witchcraft? Are there people in America today who have the magical power of witches?

Eva Watson-Jones
Warwick, Rhode Island

Dear Eva:
There are no real witches in the world, and there never *have* been. People who claim to be witches are fakes, but that doesn't mean they can't be dangerous. They can, and they are—much more than the average person. After all, anyone who even *says* he or she is a witch gives more than adequate clues to being a real *creep*, at least.

As if life in these modern United States weren't nutty enough already, have you heard that dressing up as a witch for Halloween (especially in or around Salem, Massachusetts) is now actively discouraged as being "politically incorrect"? Well, supposedly, there is a "coven" of so-called witches that raises quite a fuss there every year, complaining that the rest of us are making fun of them!

• • •

Dear Marilyn:
I received this chain letter in the mail and decided not to do as it says, mainly because I've got better things to do with the money. I'm not superstitious, but curious. Is there any truth to these letters? I'm hoping I did the right thing! I received it yesterday, so it *did* leave my hands within the ninety-six hours that it said it had to.

J. C.
Cleve, Tennessee

Dear Reader:
Don't worry about a thing. Chain letters like this are utterly meaningless. They can't give you good luck *or* bad luck, as this especially malicious one

implies, and they're nothing more than the product of an obnoxious little person somewhere who takes pleasure out of upsetting people. The next time you receive one, you can get it out of your hands by sailing it into the trashcan.

Oh, you're just not going to believe this, folks. But after that last answer appeared, I received a letter from a woman who accused me of insensitivity toward short people! (In case you have no idea what she was talking about, go back and read the reply again. See the words, "little person"?!)

● ● ●

Dear Marilyn:

I recently received a "chain" letter from a person who I had thought was intelligent enough to see the futility of it, and I refused to send it on, saying that chain letters are unproductive. This one requested that I send $1 to the top name of four, cross that name off, add my own to the bottom, and send copies to 10 people within ten days. My question is: If this chain were not broken, and limited to people in the United States, what would be the result?

Alta Crowley
Burlington, Connecticut

Dear Alta:

In less than three months, 100 million people would be staring down at chain letters that they couldn't each send to ten more people because there wouldn't be enough people left to whom the chain letter hadn't already been sent. Which would mean that they wouldn't send the money to the top names because their own names would never rise to the top of the list. Which would mean that the second names would never rise, either. And neither would the third names or the fourth names, stopping the chain.

At this point, more than $11 million would have been spent, distributed among about 1100 people, who would have received some $10,000 dollars each. If we see this as a sort of lottery, then, this would mean that your chances of "winning" $10,000 with your $1 "bet" would be about 1 in 10,000. And that's only if not a single person breaks the chain! The ethical problem arises because people don't understand the situation and think that success is assured if the chain isn't broken. That's *far* from the case.

● ● ●

Dear Marilyn:

I've written to you about this many times, but you never answer. Do you or do you not believe in UFOs?

Joey Haynes
Jacksonville, Florida

Dear Joey:

Okay, okay! Sure, there are things in the sky that we can't identify called UFOs (Unidentified Flying Objects), but there are plenty of things on the ground that we can't identify either. We don't glamorize them and call them USOs (Unidentified Sitting Objects), do we? When we look off toward the horizon at night, we're sure to see funny lights and other odd sights that we don't recognize—partly because we're not close enough and partly because it's dark—but no one believes any of them is an extraterrestrial out there on a distant bridge.

●   ●   ●

Dear Marilyn:

Do you think that if you meditate long enough, your body can rise off the ground?

Mary Ellen Graybill
Riderwood, Maryland

Dear Mary:

If your body rises off the ground, it's probably because you're finally getting thrown out of the house.

Thirty-one

Dear Marilyn:
Friends and acquaintances are unable to come up with an answer. Maybe you can. How would you describe music?

Italo Bernt
Alta Loma, California

Dear Italo:
Music is audible art. It's the stuff that sounds the way a painting looks.

● ● ●

Dear Marilyn:
Must a conductor of an orchestra be able to play all the instruments in his orchestra?

Julian Hammer
Carteret, New Jersey

Dear Julian:
This is a common myth, but no, he (or now she) certainly doesn't need to know how to play all the instruments himself—although he is always an accomplished musician and does need to be thoroughly familiar with the techniques. Historically, the most basic function of a conductor was to keep the beat for the orchestra, and he accomplished this by moving his baton. (At first, orchestras were kept together by someone maintaining an *audible* beat—such as whacking a cane against the floor, for example—but we can be thankful that this was eventually abandoned in favor of the *visible* beat.) Early on, the chore of conducting fell to composers and musicians whose primary responsibility was to perform (usually at the same time!), and perhaps this is what led to the misunderstanding.

With time, however, conducting became a specialty in itself, drawing gifted musicians with the skills necessary to deal authoritatively with this complicated task. Modern professional orchestras certainly don't need someone to note every beat, but the conductor is now of major importance both in coordinating a large assemblage of artists and achieving a unified interpretation—neither of which task requires that he be capable of playing everything from the glockenspiel to the oboe d'amore.

• • •

Dear Marilyn:
    Just recently, my wife and I attended the local symphony, and two of the pieces played were lovely, but the third was by a modern composer and sounded like just a lot of banging on the piano to me. It's crazy. Do you see anything positive in this kind of "music"?
                                                                George Dooner
                                                                Union, New Jersey

Dear George:
    Well, one good thing about some of this stuff is that at least you can't tell when the pianist has made a mistake!

• • •

Dear Marilyn:
    What is your opinion about why there are no Mozarts, Bachs, Beethovens, Chopins, Michelangelos, da Vincis, or other great creative geniuses in our time. What was it that led to the development and nurturing of these persons and others like them?
                                                                Phil and Marion Beautrow
                                                                Santa Barbara, California

Dear Phil and Marion:
    Maybe they're here already, and we just don't know it yet. Then again, public taste may be another answer, and money yet another. All those artists you mention were supported and encouraged by courts and nobility. Today, funding for the arts is extremely limited. (And in certain cases, we should be thankful!)

• • •

Dear Marilyn:
    I have long been puzzled by the acclaim given to modern paintings. To me, they appear as a collection of daubs, streaks, splashes, or meaningless

assemblages of geometric forms. Am I missing something? Do people really see "art" in these collections?

Vera Heminger
Auburn, Washington

Dear Vera:

Maybe we're *both* missing something, Vera, because it often looks that way to me, too. And we've had company as far back as the late eighteen hundreds, when the first stirrings of modern art were felt, and Paris was the art center of the Western world. At that time, nearly every French art critic ridiculed even the now-accepted Impressionists as little more than a group of incompetents who thought that publicity stunts might be a substitute for the talent they didn't have.

Thirty-two

T H E   P E R S O N A L S

Dear Marilyn:

I love your name. It's too good to be true! Is "vos Savant" really your family name, or is it a pen name?

> Sally Jensen
> North Syracuse, New York

Is your last name a joke? Doesn't "savant" mean "wise" or "genius"?

> J. Beasley
> Traverse City, Michigan

I find it hard to believe that your name is actually "Savant," for obvious reasons.

> Hiawatha
> Eugene, Oregon

Dear Readers:

I give up! I answered this question a few years ago and have refrained from answering it again in order not to repeat myself. However, because not everyone saw that particular reply, and I receive a constant stream of letters on the subject, I'll say it another time.

To the first two readers: My last name is not a pen name. It's my mother's maiden name, and the name "Savant" appears independently twice among my immediate ancestors. My maternal grandmother's maiden name was Mary Savant, and my maternal grandfather's name was Joseph vos Savant. And to the third reader: With a name like yours, you shouldn't be talking, fella.

However, when I received this next letter, I began to wish I did use a pen name!

Dear Marilyn:

I look forward to your column every Sunday. I don't know if you do such things, but I sure would enjoy an autographed picture. It doesn't hurt to ask. If not, I understand.

Larry Williams
Poestenkill, New York

Dear Larry:

Good heavens, Larry. I can understand an employee of the Department of Motor Vehicles asking for a photo, but did you have to attach your note to my renewed driver's license?! And after seeing *that* photo, I'm surprised you wanted to ask at all. I look like the "before" half of a vitamin ad. But maybe that's not surprising, given the fact that I'd stood in line for two hours beforehand. After all, there is just *one* line for all of Manhattan down at the Department of Motor Vehicles. One line! (Oh, but there are several windows. Several! For a million and a half souls!) And at the *front* of the line, obscured by hundreds of people, was a little sign—"Please bring two forms of identification with you."

•   •   •

Dear Marilyn:

I read that you're not too happy with your first name because it reminds you of another Marilyn—Marilyn Monroe. How does it feel being compared to her?

Jeannie D.
St. Charles, Illinois

Dear Jeannie:

Well, no one has confused us yet, Jeannie! But how does it feel? It feels like going through life wearing a pair of new shoes.

•   •   •

Dear Marilyn:

Believe it or not, I have a picture of you in your gym suit during your sophomore year of high school! Want it back?

William Sharp
San Diego, California

Dear William:

Do me a favor, William—don't send it here. If I were you, I'd just stick it on the end of a pole and put it out in the garden. It may scare a few crows away.

• • •

Dear Marilyn:

Did you ever want to skip a grade because you thought you were smarter than the teacher?

Lisa Irons
Kenner, Louisiana

Dear Lisa:

No. What would that have to do with skipping a grade? But I never thought I was smarter than the teacher, anyway. Just because a youngster occasionally finds a new way to solve a problem has virtually no effect on the teaching relationship. In elementary school especially, darned near any teacher knows about a zillion times as much as darned near any kid.

• • •

Dear Marilyn:
What is most often wrongly assumed about you?

Randy Lynn Rutledge
Bakersfield, California

Dear Randy:

That I can "perform," as in rapid calculation, feats of memory, or recitation of arcane data. (If I'm desperate, I can tap-dance a little, though.)

• • •

Dear Marilyn:

What do you think about in your spare time? Do you think about mundane things such as recipes, landscaping, or the weather? Or is most of your thinking devoted to such things as analyzing, evaluating, and problem-solving?

B. Crumpton
Brandon, Florida

Dear Reader:

Goodness! Do I look like a human computer? Late in the afternoon, I begin thinking mainly about dinner; during dinner, I like to think about politics; and after dinner, I try to avoid thinking at all.

• • •

Dear Marilyn:
Do you cook?

J. Ekelman
Mount Clemens, Michigan

Dear Reader:
  No. But it's for humanitarian reasons. (I save lives that way.)

• • •

Dear Marilyn:
  How tall are you?

D. S.
Eugene, Oregon

Dear Reader:
  I'm five-feet-eight and seldom find clothes long enough. I'm not that tall, for heaven's sake, but women's clothes are usually too short for my taste. As far as I'm concerned, skirts come in only three different lengths: ballroom, business, and bimbo.

Interestingly, that last line drew a positive response from men, but a negative response from a few women. Sounds like there's a little sartorial miscommunication going on here! At any rate, I replied to one more letter about the subject.

Dear Marilyn:
  You mentioned that "skirts come in only three different lengths: ballroom, business, and bimbo." We are having some difficulty defining "bimbo" and look to you for assistance.

Bob B. and Mike W.
Southbridge, Massachusetts

Dear Bob and Mike:
  Glad you asked, guys. A "bimbo" is a man who wears a revealing shirt and short pants when he wants to look his best because he believes that his chest and legs are among his most important assets, that it's advantageous for a man to look "sexy" (without looking cheap, of course), and that men who think otherwise are either guilty of stereotyping, old-fashioned prudes, or just plain envious of his nice knees.
  (P. S. There are female "bimbos," too.)

• • •

Dear Marilyn:
  Do you usually answer with your first thought?

Roberta Edgington
Crown Point, Indiana

Dear Roberta:

Goodness, no. My thoughts are like waffles—the first few don't look too good.

• • •

Dear Marilyn:

Forgive my ignorance, but what exactly is meant by the sentence, "Personal replies are not possible," that appears at the end of your column? Do people write only with the hope that their questions will be seen in the magazine? (If so, their questions aren't answered otherwise!)

Mark Grasak
Decatur, Alabama

Dear Mark:

"Not possible" means that even if I were to stop eating and sleeping, I could *still* come nowhere near answering all the questions sent to me. As it is, I am submerged in mail, and it requires not just the complex machinery of the magazine itself, but my own personal assistant to extricate me daily.

But if you don't see your question appear, all is not lost. You should write again. And perhaps phrase the question a bit differently; that is, define it a little more clearly. Or send another question entirely. Surely there's more than one issue on your mind! But how tough can it be, anyway, Mark? You saw *your* question appear, didn't you?!

• • •

Dear Marilyn:

What determines which questions will be answered in your column? I've submitted many letters to you with a particular question, and you have yet to answer it. ("Which is faster, the speed of light or the speed of thought?")

Nelson Hall
Vauxhall, New Jersey

Dear Nelson:

It's determined by serendipity, a word that comes from the Persian fairy tale called "The Three Princes of Serendip," in which characters possess a trait that leads them to make fortunate (and unexpected) discoveries by accident. (But maybe it's time to try a new question, Nelson. Yes, that's a hint!)

• • •

Dear Marilyn:

Why don't you respond to all your letters?

Bobby of Grosskoff
Corpus Christi, Texas

Dear Bobby:

Clearly, you've never seen our mailroom! There are only two situations in which columnists can reply to all their letters: One, if they don't get many, or two, if they use form letters.

I think I might be capable of personally replying to as many as two-dozen letters a day if I had nothing else to do in life. But I get far more than that, of course, and I *do* have other things to do. And as far as form letters are concerned, have you ever tried signing your name a hundred times in the morning? How about *every* morning?

●   ●   ●

Dear Marilyn:

It seems impossible that you write this column yourself, answering questions that are mathematical, scientific, and philosophical. Do you have a team of professionals helping you?

B. T.
Pittsburgh, Pennsylvania

Dear Reader:

No. But I do have a nice young man as an editorial assistant, and he serves every function from answering the telephone to throwing up his hands in despair when the mailman approaches.

●   ●   ●

Dear Marilyn:

What's the most important answer that you've ever given?

Huey Tate
Maurice, Louisiana

Dear Huey:

"Yes." (You should have asked me what the question was, too, Huey.)

●   ●   ●

Dear Marilyn:

Does your husband help you with these questions? (Please do not use my name.)

Anonymous
Chickasaw, Alabama

Dear Reader:

No. When he's not in the laboratory, he's usually far too busy cooking. (And for your own protection, sir, I would have removed your name myself.)

However, my husband does use his considerable influence on occasion, such as with the following letter.

Dear Marilyn:
    Did I read somewhere years ago that you had married that gorgeous Dr. Jarvik, who invented the Jarvik-7 artificial heart? Are you still married to him, you lucky woman?

Barbara Presley
Atlanta, Georgia

Yes. In fact, he's looking over my shoulder right now, Barbara, making sure I don't forget to include your letter in this book.

Part Five

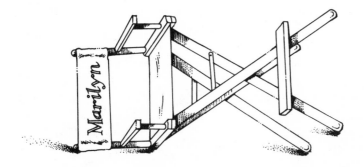

Thirty-three

Dear Marilyn:
    I know your higher intelligence makes you superior in problem-solving, mathematics, science, and social questions. The problem is this: My car needs a transmission overhaul. The last man I had do one charged $460. Can you overhaul my transmission for a reasonable price?

                                                        B. P.
                                                        Antioch, Illinois

●   ●   ●

Dear Marilyn:
    In the Garden of Eden, after God created Adam and before Eve was created, did Adam have sex organs? If he did, what for? If he didn't, did God have to go back and "fix" Adam?

                                                        M. L. M.
                                                        Shippensburg, Pennsylvania

●   ●   ●

Dear Marilyn:
    We hear so much about global warming these days, but would it accomplish any good if all the world's governments required citizens to turn on all their air conditioners in their homes and offices and cars (on a specific day) and open all their doors and windows?

                                                        M.
                                                        New Orleans, Louisiana

●   ●   ●

Dear Marilyn:
    Why is he called the Lone Ranger if Tonto is always with him?

                                                        J. H.
                                                        Vaughn, Washington

• • •

Dear Marilyn:
This evening while enjoying the cool air outside, I noticed the crescent moon upon the picturesque sky. Then it occurred to me, what if the moon were wiped out as if it were an unwanted object in a painting? That is, what would happen if several hydrogen bombs exploded on its surface during the Fourth of July? Wouldn't that be a spectacle? Of course, we wouldn't want anyone to get hurt.

M. T. R.
Bellevue, Washington

• • •

Dear Marilyn:
A fast-food chain offers on its menu a muffin (raisin or raspberry). The problem is how to cut these muffins in half in order to eat them. The establishment serves butter and a plastic knife, but no instructions. The obvious way to cut these muffins is up to down in the center. This way you have two equal halves to butter and enjoy. My request is that you straighten the other people out—officially—who insist on cutting these muffins from side to side in the center to end up with two unequal parts. These people, unless stopped now, will be going through their whole stupid lives eating tops and bottoms rather than halves. I think they are all very bullheaded and probably vote Democratic. Please publish this with a qualified answer before this leads to something bigger.

J. K.
Abingdon, Illinois

• • •

Dear Marilyn:
I would appreciate any information on where to purchase an electric pop rivet gun.

J. L. T.
Addis, Louisiana

• • •

Dear Marilyn:
What happens to gum after it is disposed of? Does it rot away, or does it stay on Earth forever?

S. A.
Frankenmuth, Michigan

• • •

Dear Marilyn:

I have been trying for more than a year to get Powdered Dancing Wax, but nobody has heard of it. Will you please help me?

C. E. C.
Portland, Oregon

• • •

Dear Marilyn:

I would like to raise my I.Q. Do you think bifocals would help? I would also like to be a politician. (P.S. How can I get into a think tank?)

P. B.
North Plainfield, New Jersey

• • •

Dear Marilyn:

I was very good in geography from grade school through high school. As far as I know, there is only one world. Who came up with the bright idea of a Third World, and what happened to the "second world," if there was one?

R. F. W.
Salt Lake City, Utah

• • •

Dear Marilyn:

My husband used to sing these lines (if you could call it singing): "O Captain, my Captain stood on a burning deck. O Captain, my Captain I have cream puffs in my shoes." Never any other lines. Now and then I think about them and wonder if they're from a poem or song, or was it just something he made up?

M. E. W.
Phoenix, Arizona

• • •

Dear Marilyn:

How come so many squirrels are killed crossing the street? Don't they know how to cross?

J. H.
Carteret, New Jersey

• • •

Dear Marilyn:
Hypothetical question: In one fell swoop, God removes the thumbs of every man, woman and child on Earth! What do you believe would be the major immediate, short-term, and long-term effects?

C. W. S.
Newport News, Virginia

• • •

Dear Marilyn:
You still haven't answered my questions about oranges and the cable system. I have some other questions that I don't think you have the answers to: What are we going to do when all of our "landfills" are full? Where is our clean water going to come from when our "dumps" have contaminated all our wells? Those are my questions, Marilyn. Forget about the oranges and the cable-system questions. If you can answer these, you will have done a good enough job.

J. E. N.
Murion, Ohio

• • •

Dear Marilyn:
I enjoy your column and decided to tap into your expertise with the following question: How many mosquitoes would it take to suck all the blood from an individual's body at one time?

P. E. B.
Canton, Ohio

• • •

Dear Marilyn:
I often read your column, and once in a while I am disappointed with the questions you choose to answer because I consider them trivial, not worthy of your intellect, but there are others that really show your brilliance. Maybe this will stump you, but I'm including a question that has intrigued me for some time. I hope you can give me a serious answer: Why don't the Chinese use potatoes in their food?

H. C.
Tampa, Florida

● ● ●

Dear Marilyn:
 Why is our Right side not called Left and our Left side not called Right?
Why?

F. O.
Torrington, Connecticut

● ● ●

Dear Marilyn:
 If you read Bibles, which Bible do you prefer?
 I'm related to lumber.
 Who sold Noah (of Noah's Ark) the lumber? Or was it a contribution?

M.
Lincoln, Nebraska

● ● ●

Dear Marilyn:
 Since there were only seven wonders of the world, and only one is still in existence, namely the pyramids, how does Donald Trump get away with using "The Eighth Wonder of the World" in his commercial for his Taj Mahal casino? Isn't this in violation of some international edict?

J. K.
Woodbridge, New Jersey

● ● ●

Dear Marilyn:
 During the last Olympic Games, one contestant in the diving competition did a series of spins in the air and then straightened out into a plain old belly flop! Wouldn't that have been a lot less painful if the pool had been filled with "soft water"?

G. A. G.
Portland, Oregon

● ● ●

Dear Marilyn:
 I have two boys, and both have very white hair. Several of our older friends call them "toe heads." Can you tell me what that means and where the term originated?

C. L. F.
La Crosse, Wisconsin

● ● ●

Dear Marilyn:

My question concerns the lipstick on models and movie stars in magazine photos. Why does it stray so far outside the lines of the lips? Do they think this looks good? Do they think we're blind? Stupid? Or what?

R. C.
Whitesburg, Kentucky

● ● ●

Dear Marilyn:

Have there been any biographies written about King Brian Boro, ruler in Ireland, 976–1014? The books I've found only mention him briefly!

M. G.
Warner Robins, Georgia

● ● ●

Dear Marilyn:

Can your teeth sweat?

J. H.
Carteret, New Jersey

● ● ●

Dear Marilyn:

It seems to me that you must really be lacking material for your column when you choose to print some asinine letter about someone eating corn on the cob into a perfect square. I wrote you a letter over two weeks ago asking a real and pertinent question, yet you have chosen to ignore it: Why are manhole covers round? I'm making copies of this letter, and I'll send one to you every week until I see it in print.

B. B. B.
Aurora, Colorado

Okay, you can stop now! (You never said I had to answer it.)

● ● ●

Dear Marilyn:

I've heard that television adds ten pounds to your usual body weight. Why and where?

B. K.
Los Angeles, California

● ● ●

Dear Marilyn:
   A madman of average height and weight is rapping "Shave and a Haircut" on an iron door at a rate of a hundred times a minute. Assuming that this activity destroys brain cells, how long would it take for him to die?

C. M.
Washington, D. C.

● ● ●

Dear Marilyn:
   If a piece of bread with butter on it falls, it will always land butter-side down. When a cat falls, it will always land on its feet. If you tied a piece of buttered bread to a cat's back and let both fall, which side would end up on the floor? Or would the buttered side of the bread slip around to the cat's stomach?

B.
Forest Lake, Minnesota

● ● ●

Dear Marilyn:
   Do you have any idea why young men like to wear their baseball caps backwards?

T. C.
Memphis, Tennessee

Hmmm. Maybe their caps are on forward, and their brains are in backward.

● ● ●

Dear Marilyn:
   If Fred Flintstone knew that the large order of ribs would tip over his car, why did he order them every day?

D. W.
Arlington, Texas

● ● ●

Dear Marilyn:
   You know everything. How many parts does a typical automobile have? In particular, how many parts does a two-door 1979 Honda Accord (with power steering and air conditioning) have?

D. E.
Houston, Texas

What color is it?

• • •

Dear Marilyn:
How many cans of chicken noodle soup does it take to use up one chicken?
                                          P. S.
                                          Holton, Michigan

• • •

Dear Marilyn:
I have two questions to ask you that I've been trying to figure out for ages: "Is there life after death?" and "How can quick-dry spray make your nails dry quicker?"
                                          J. C.
                                          West New York, New Jersey

• • •

Dear Marilyn:
How come the Lord wanted us to have gums? Is there a significant reason for having gums?
                                          S. C.
                                          Brooklyn, New York

• • •

Dear Marilyn:
Why does a fly die when it's hit with a flyswatter?
                                          A. N.
                                          Lakeland, Florida

• • •

Dear Marilyn:
Has there been a change in the calendar system since 1955? My nephew was born on March 5, 1955, and his mother and I know he was born on a Friday. The library says March 5, 1955, was a Saturday.
                                          E. R. J.
                                          St. Louis, Missouri

● ● ●

Dear Marilyn:
   Why do ducks have orange feet? This question came up in a conversation a couple of years ago, and no one seems to know the reason. Especially since geese have black feet. Please help clear this up.
                                                                    C. J. S.
                                                                    Reston, Virginia

● ● ●

Dear Marilyn:
   H_2O = water. Why can't people manufacture it? The formula seems simple enough.
                                                                    E. F. R.
                                                                    Fresno, California

● ● ●

Dear Marilyn:
   Why don't male basketball players shave their underarms like female basketball players?
                                                                    W. V.
                                                                    Fresno, California

● ● ●

Dear Marilyn:
   Not being a mathematical genius, I usually pass on your brainteasers, but I would be interested in knowing the odds of my pistol-grip hose nozzle squirting me in the face when I drop it while washing the car. It seems like 100 percent.
                                                                    C. S. B.
                                                                    Kernville, California

● ● ●

Dear Marilyn:
   If a chicken lays an egg, and the farmer takes the egg and hatches it in an incubator, does the chicken become a mother when the egg hatches? If the hen goes to the hatchery and pokes a hole or two in the egg so the egg cannot hatch, does the farmer have a right to be angry at the chicken? I think he does. Surely after having raised, fed, and got the hen a rooster so she could produce the farmer a chick, he has the right to expect some return for his loving care. Besides, I like chicken for dinner.

Another observation: I have noted that a chicken cannot be raped. If she is not prepared for impregnation, she just walks away from the male, and when she accepts him, she is in a very awkward position and gives no indication that she (1) enjoys it, (2) does it willingly, or (3) wishes some other rooster in the yard were doing it. I don't know how the hen feels about the whole thing, but I do know the result. She lays a fertilized egg that can produce another chicken. So—back to the question—is the chicken a momma or not?

A. V. O. M.
Vienna, Virginia

• • •

Dear Marilyn:
If someone says his or her vacuum cleaner really sucks, does that mean the vacuum is in good condition or poor condition?

S. W.
Warner Springs, California

• • •

Dear Marilyn:
What are the chances that we will one day colonize Mars? If and when we do, what will children born there be called—Earthlings or Martians? Also, what size shoe do you wear?

B. G.
Corpus Christi, Texas

• • •

Dear Marilyn:
Given that tissue seat-covers have largely disappeared from ladies' restrooms since I was a kid, and I've used public restrooms in about thirty countries, about how many tushes would you say I've "communed" with?

K. F.
Silver Spring, Maryland

• • •

Dear Marilyn:
Should they be testing chess players for steroids?

G. A. G.
Portland, Oregon

Maybe that's *what gave Bobby Fischer such a big head for a while.*

● ● ●

Dear Marilyn:
 Could you please tell me what happened to the man who used to advertise washing machines? His line was, "I'm the loneliest man in town." The machines supposedly never needed repairs.
                                            A. P.
                                            New Port Richey, Florida

● ● ●

Dear Marilyn:
 Why do baseball players spit so much? Football players don't. Basketball players don't. Soccer players don't.
                                            J. S. P.
                                            Savannah, Georgia

● ● ●

Dear Marilyn:
 What causes apparently normal people of various age, color, and creed to cruise in the passing lane of our nation's highway system?
                                            R. K.
                                            Osprey, Florida

● ● ●

Dear Marilyn:
 Just in case you thought I was trying to be "cute" in a previous letter, I'm writing again to let you know that I would sincerely and seriously like you to tell me which should be done first—dusting the furniture or vacuuming the carpet? And why?
                                            B. J.
                                            Rogersville, Tennessee

● ● ●

Dear Marilyn:
 Why do goats have such strange eyes?
                                            E. B.
                                            Lexington, Kentucky

• • •

Dear Marilyn:
Why is it that if I have a hole in one sock at my big toe and then move that sock to my other foot, the hole is still at my big toe and not at my little toe, the way I expected?

M. H.
Vale, North Carolina

• • •

Dear Marilyn:
Will you please explain how and why cockroaches turn over on their backs when they die?

F. E. J.
New Orleans, Louisiana

• • •

Dear Marilyn:
How come your grocery cart always goes to the left?

J. H.
Carteret, New Jersey

• • •

Dear Marilyn:
What are the odds of a person in Michigan getting dumped on by a bird? How does getting hit by a bird dropping compare to getting hit by lightning, automobiles, lawn rakes, and any other useful statistics you may feel we in Michigan should know for safety reasons?

J. S.
Bay City, Michigan

• • •

Dear Marilyn:
Would you please suggest to someone involved in cotton-diaper production that single-use diapers could be washed and dried in the sun, then used to mop up oil spills.

A.
Bakersfield, California

• • •

Dear Marilyn:

I would like to know why flies can find their way into a house through an open window, but if you leave the window open, they can't ever find their way back out.

J. A.
Portland, Maine

• • •

Dear Marilyn:

Do you think it's possible to get bad eyestrain from watching a full-blown nightmare without your glasses?

E. R.
San Diego, California

• • •

Dear Marilyn:

Who is responsible for words like "coruscate" and why?

T. M.
Gassville, Arkansas

• • •

Dear Marilyn:

How much dander can fly off a parrot when he flutters or flaps his wings during a four- to five-second episode? Or how much dander is this over a one-hour period if he flaps every ten minutes?

V. M. D.
Whitehall, Pennsylvania

• • •

Dear Marilyn:

Please settle an argument: Are there still only fifty states in the United States? Or have a few more been added?

S. B.
Amarillo, Texas

• • •

Dear Marilyn:

If humans use cow's milk for themselves, what do the cows use to feed their young?

D. L.
Astoria, New York

• • •

Dear Marilyn:
Please answer this pressing question so I can carry on with my life: Is the English language a constant, or can it be revised in time? I feel much better now. Thank you.

T. H. S.
Camp LeJeune, North Carolina

• • •

Dear Marilyn:
If you have any questions on motorcycles, I could help. However, due to the volume of mail I receive, please limit your correspondence to seven pages.

J. J. K.
Ann Arbor, Michigan

• • •

Dear Marilyn:
If we don't like a smell, we spray it with a deodorant. Why don't we just spray some glitter on a sight we don't like to see?

F. M.
Columbus, Georgia

• • •

Dear Marilyn:
How or why is it that no matter how they are placed in a tumble dryer, cotton underwear panties always turn wrong-side out?

T. L. C.
Revere, Massachusetts

• • •

Dear Marilyn:
Could you tell me how a man becomes his own grandmother? (P.S. It's mind-boggling, and I think that the man committed suicide when he found out.)

S. H.
Overland, Missouri

• • •

Dear Marilyn:
  Some railroad locomotives are equipped with four-by-thirty-six-inch electric-heating elements. Will my can of chicken noodle soup heat faster if I place it on the heater straight up or if I lay the can on its side?
                                              J. A. M.
                                              Youngstown, Ohio

• • •

Dear Marilyn:
  When the "Answer Man" retired several years ago, he said there were only two questions he couldn't answer: Do mosquitoes dream, and how many buffaloes would it take to fill the Grand Canyon? Can you answer these?
                                              M. M.
                                              Chapel Hill, North Carolina

• • •

Dear Marilyn:
  You have a beautiful smile, and I guess you practice good dental hygiene. Do you floss? I do, but not in restaurants.
                                              S. C.
                                              Brooklyn, New York

• • •

Dear Marilyn:
  On many products, "natural flavoring" is listed as an ingredient. What is natural flavoring, and where can I get a bottle of it?
                                              S. P.
                                              Upper Marlboro, Maryland

• • •

Dear Marilyn:
  I am not a cannibal, but I was wondering about something. Everybody says that if you don't eat the skin on the chicken, you'll save a lot of calories. Well, I sometimes nibble the skin around my nail (just out of habit). Are there also calories in our dead skin just as there are with chickens' dead skin?
                                              A.
                                              St. Petersburg, Florida

•   •   •

Dear Marilyn:

I wonder if you can explain why one spare tire can be placed on either the right or left side of a car, but if we needed spare ears, we would need right and left spares. What difference in shape between wheels and ears accounts for this?

G. W. K.
Tequesta, Florida

•   •   •

Dear Marilyn:

Do you really breathe out of one nostril at a time?

C. T.
South Portland, Maine

•   •   •

Dear Marilyn:

How can a black-and-white cow eat green grass and give white milk?

J. N.
Bay City, Michigan

•   •   •

Dear Marilyn:

In a freak accident, I recently hit myself in the eye with a racquet while attempting to return a volley. Does this mean that I subconsciously hate myself?

M. B.
Birmingham, Alabama

•   •   •

Dear Marilyn:

I have two questions for you based on the supposition that all your body functions stop when you sneeze: (1) Will you live longer if you sneeze a lot? (2) If so, do you think I could make any money selling a sneezing powder to make you live longer?

B. J.
Jacksonville, Florida

• • •

Dear Marilyn:
If your knees bent the other way, what would a chair look like?
M. B.
Irving, Texas

• • •

Dear Marilyn:
If a vampire weighing, say, 160 pounds, changes to a bat that weighs only one pound, what happens to the 159 pounds that did not take flight with the bat?
B. H.
Richmond, Virginia

• • •

Dear Marilyn:
If there really is a heaven and a hell, then why do we bury most people in the ground—closer to hell?
J. R.
Greensboro, North Carolina

• • •

Dear Marilyn:
I have always been very attracted to highly intelligent women, and you are most certainly one of the most attractive women I have ever seen. Would you please be so kind as to have a CAT scan done and send me a "centerfold" of your brain?
D. B.
Kansas City, Missouri

• • •

Dear Marilyn:
Did you inherit your high I.Q. from your parents, or were you born with it?
W. T. M.
Rutland, Vermont

• • •

Dear Marilyn:

Please send me free information on questions for Marilyn vos Savant.

K. K.
Shelton, Washington

```
┌─────────────────────────────────────────┐
│                                           │
│         Do you have a question?           │
│             Send it to:                   │
│                                           │
│                                           │
│      ASK MARILYN VOS SAVANT               │
│          Ansonia Station                  │
│        Post Office Box 967                │
│      New York, New York 10023             │
│                                           │
└─────────────────────────────────────────┘
```

Because of the volume of mail, we regret that personal replies will not be possible.

ABOUT "ASK MARILYN" READERS

The "Ask Marilyn" corner of the *Parade* mailroom is just about the most quintessentially American place you can find anywhere. Open letters at random, and you'll find a note from a curious child, a technical paper from a bright amateur mathematician, a critique from a helpful university professor, a dissertation on life, love, truth, and beauty from a frustrated philosopher, a batch of funny riddles from a men's poker club, a photograph of little old ladies playing bingo, a box of jigsaw puzzles, audiotapes, video-tapes, computer diskettes, and a pair of socks. Multiply that charm and diversity by several hundred each week, and you get the idea of what it's like. And I love it all.

So it's tough to profile "Ask Marilyn" readers, and I won't even try, except to mention that a sizable percentage of them are male. I do get an occasional marriage proposal and other romantic gestures—along with cards, flowers, candy, and . . . a box of tools. (Don't ask.) I'm flattered, but I'm already married. (Then again, so are many of the people who propose to me!) We also have people who write regularly, some more than once a week, but many people open their letters with, "I've never written to a columnist before . . ."

It would be impossible to respond to everyone personally, and I don't like to send form letters, so let me take this opportunity to let you know that if you've written to me, I've seen your letter, and your voice has been heard. Goodbye for now, and to the rest of you out there, don't forget to write!

INDEX OF LETTER-WRITERS BY TOWN AND STATE

Marilyn vos Savant was born in St. Louis, Missouri, the daughter of Mary vos Savant and Joseph Mach. She is married to Robert Jarvik, M.D., the inventor of the Jarvik-7 artificial heart. They live in Manhattan. Marilyn vos Savant was listed in the *Guinness Book of World Records* for five years under "Highest I. Q." for both childhood and adult scores, and she has now been inducted into the Guinness Hall of Fame. She is a writer and lecturer, and she spends additional time assisting her husband in the artificial heart program. Her special interests and concerns are quality education and humanitarian medical research. She describes herself as an "independent" with regard to politics and religion, and only an "armchair" feminist.

Marilyn vos Savant writes the "Ask Marilyn" question-and-answer problem-analysis column for *Parade*, the Sunday magazine for more than 352 newspapers nationwide, with a circulation of 36 million and a readership of 70 million, the largest in the world. Future book publications include: *Ask Marilyn*, to be published in a mass-market edition and *Number Blindness*, to be published in hardcover, both by St. Martin's Press. Past book publications include: *"I've Forgotten Everything I Learned in School!"* published in hardcover; *The World's Most Famous Math Problem: The Proof of Fermat's Last Theorem and Other Mathematical Mysteries* published in trade paperback; and *Ask Marilyn* published in both hardcover and paperback, all by St. Martin's Press.

Her stage play called *It Was Poppa's Will* was produced in staged readings. She also has written a fantasy/satire (novel) of a dozen classical civilizations in history called *The Re-Creation* and a futuristic political fantasy/satire (novel) called *The New Patriot*.

But far from being the stereotype of the intellectual, vos Savant says she believes that "an ounce of sequins is worth a pound of home cooking," adding that she doesn't engage in the latter "for humanitarian reasons." And what does she do for fun? Read a book? Retreat to the wilderness? She looks surprised. "Not at all. My idea of fun is going out with people," she says. "A park is a nice place to visit, but I wouldn't want to live there. I'd rather be surrounded by a thousand people than a thousand trees." Her hobby is writing letters to friends around the world.